An English Guide to Kamakura's Temples & Shrines

by **Kenji Kamio**
and **Heather Willson**

緑風出版

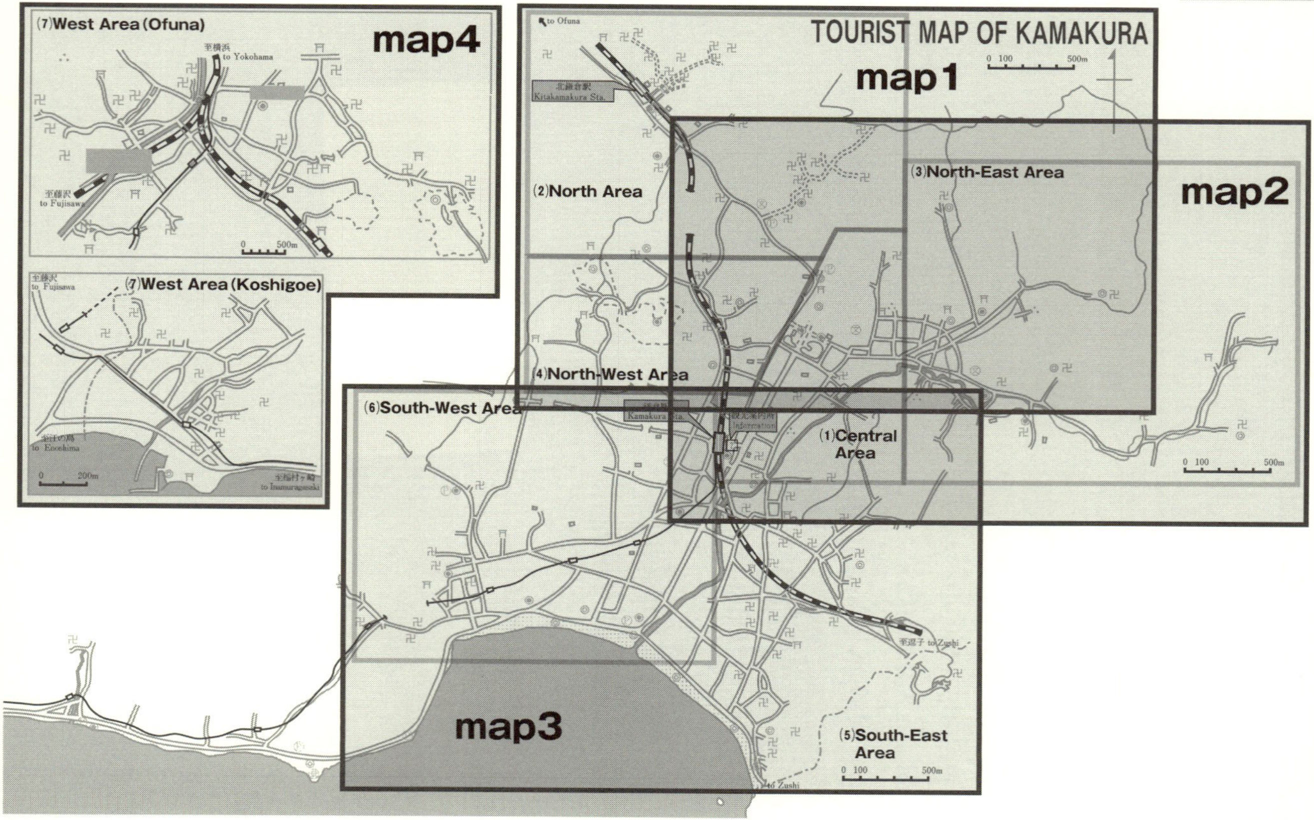
TOURIST MAP OF KAMAKURA
map1
map2
map3
map4
(1)Central Area
(2)North Area
(3)North-East Area
(4)North-West Area
(5)South-East Area
(6)South-West Area
(7)West Area (Ofuna)
(7)West Area (Koshigoe)
to Ofuna
北鎌倉駅
Kitakamakura Sta.
Kamakura Sta.
至横浜
to Yokohama
至藤沢
to Fujisawa
至逗子 to Zushi
to Zushi
to Enoshima
to Inamuragasaki
0 100 500m
0 200m

TOURIST MAP OF KAMAKURA

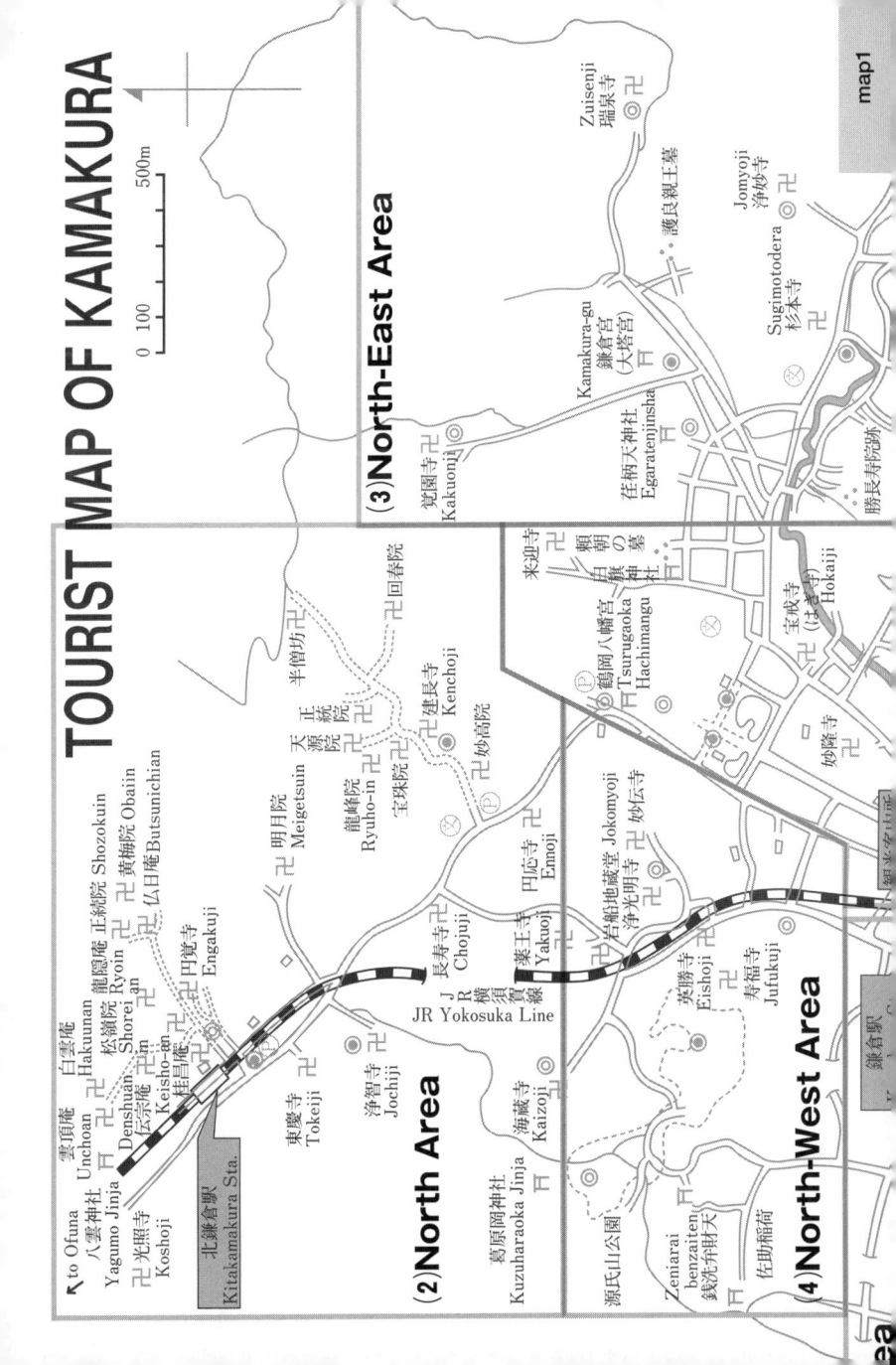

0 100 500m

(3) North-East Area

- 瑞泉寺 Zuisenji
- 浄妙寺 Jomyoji
- 鎌倉宮(大塔宮) Kamakura-gu
- 護良親王墓
- 杉本寺 Sugimotodera
- 荏柄天神社 Egaratenjinsha
- 勝長寿院跡
- 覚園寺 Kakuonji

(2) North Area

- 雲頂庵 Unchoan
- 白雲庵 Hakuunan
- 八雲神社 Yagumo Jinja
- 光照寺 Koshoji
- 龍隠庵 Denshuan
- 正続院 Shozokuin
- 松嶺院 Shorei-an
- 黄梅院 Obaiin
- 仏日庵 Butsunichian
- 佛嶺庵
- 桂昌庵 Keisho-an
- 円覚寺 Engakuji
- 明月院 Meigetsuin
- 天源院
- 正統院
- 半僧坊
- 回春院
- 建長寺 Kenchoji
- 龍峰院 Ryuho-in
- 宝珠院
- 妙高院
- 東慶寺 Tokeiji
- 浄智寺 Jochiji
- 長寿寺 Chojuji
- JR横須賀線 JR Yokosuka Line
- 円応寺 Ennoji
- 薬王寺 Yakuoji
- 岩船地蔵堂
- 浄光明寺 Jokomyoji
- 妙伝寺
- 鶴岡八幡宮 Tsurugaoka Hachimangu
- 頼朝の墓
- 白旗神社
- 来迎寺
- 宝戒寺(萩寺) Hokaiji
- 妙隆寺

Kitakamakura Sta. 北鎌倉駅

(4) North-West Area

- 葛原岡神社 Kuzuharaoka Jinja
- 海蔵寺 Kaizoji
- 源氏山公園
- 銭洗弁財天 Zeniarai benzaiten
- 佐助稲荷
- 英勝寺 Eishoji
- 寿福寺 Jufukuji

鎌倉駅

to Ofuna

map1

map2

(3) North-East Area

(1) Central Area

卍 光触寺 Kosokuji

十二社神社 Juniso Jinja

明王院 卍 Meioin

瑞泉寺 Zuisenji

護良親王墓

浄妙寺 Jomyoji

杉本寺 Sugimotodera

報国寺(竹の寺) Hokokuji

鎌倉宮(大塔宮) Kamakura-gu

荏柄天神社 Egaratenjinsha

勝長寿院跡

覚園寺 Kakuonji

来迎寺

頼朝墓
白旗神社

明月院 Meigetsuin

半僧坊

正統院
天源院

回春院

龍峰院
Ryuho-in

宝珠院

建長寺 Kenchoji

妙高院

鶴岡八幡宮 Tsurugaoka Hachimangu

宝戒寺 Hokaiji

妙隆寺

妙本寺 Myohonji

大宝寺

常栄寺
八雲神社

別願寺 安養院

円応寺 Ennoji

岩船地蔵堂 浄光明寺 浄妙寺 妙伝寺
Jokomyoji

長寿寺 Chojuji

薬王寺 Yakuoji

英勝寺 Eishoji
寿福寺 Jufukuji

観光案内所 Information

大巧寺

本覚寺

歓喜寺

延...

JR 横須賀線 JR Yokosuka Line

Sta.

0 100 500m

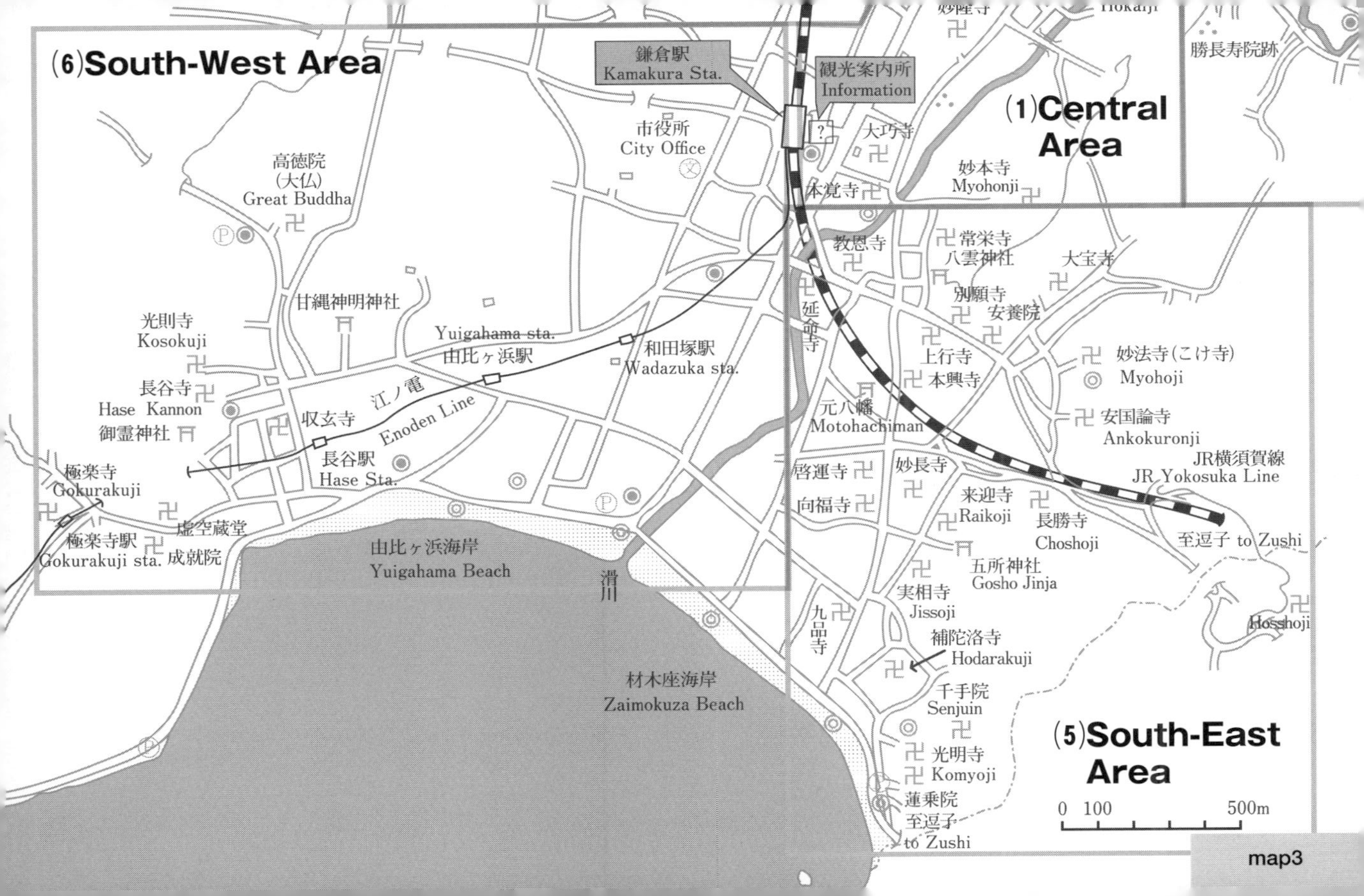

(6)South-West Area
鎌倉駅
Kamakura Sta.
観光案内所
Information
(1)Central
Area
勝長寿院跡
大巧寺
妙本寺
Myohonji
本覚寺
市役所
City Office
高徳院
(大仏)
Great Buddha
教恩寺
常栄寺
八雲神社
大宝寺
別願寺
安養院
延命寺
上行寺
本興寺
妙法寺(こけ寺)
Myohoji
安国論寺
Ankokuronji
元八幡
Motohachiman
JR横須賀線
JR Yokosuka Line
甘縄神明神社
光則寺
Kosokuji
Yuigahama sta.
由比ヶ浜駅
和田塚駅
Wadazuka sta.
長谷寺
Hase Kannon
御霊神社
収玄寺
江ノ電
Enoden Line
長谷駅
Hase Sta.
極楽寺
Gokurakuji
虚空蔵堂
極楽寺駅
Gokurakuji sta.
成就院
由比ヶ浜海岸
Yuigahama Beach
滑川
材木座海岸
Zaimokuza Beach
啓運寺
妙長寺
向福寺
来迎寺
Raikoji
長勝寺
Choshoji
至逗子 to Zushi
五所神社
Gosho Jinja
実相寺
Jissoji
九品寺
補陀洛寺
Hodarakuji
Hosshoji
千手院
Senjuin
(5)South-East
Area
光明寺
Komyoji
蓮乗院
至逗子
to Zushi
0 100 500m
map3

map4

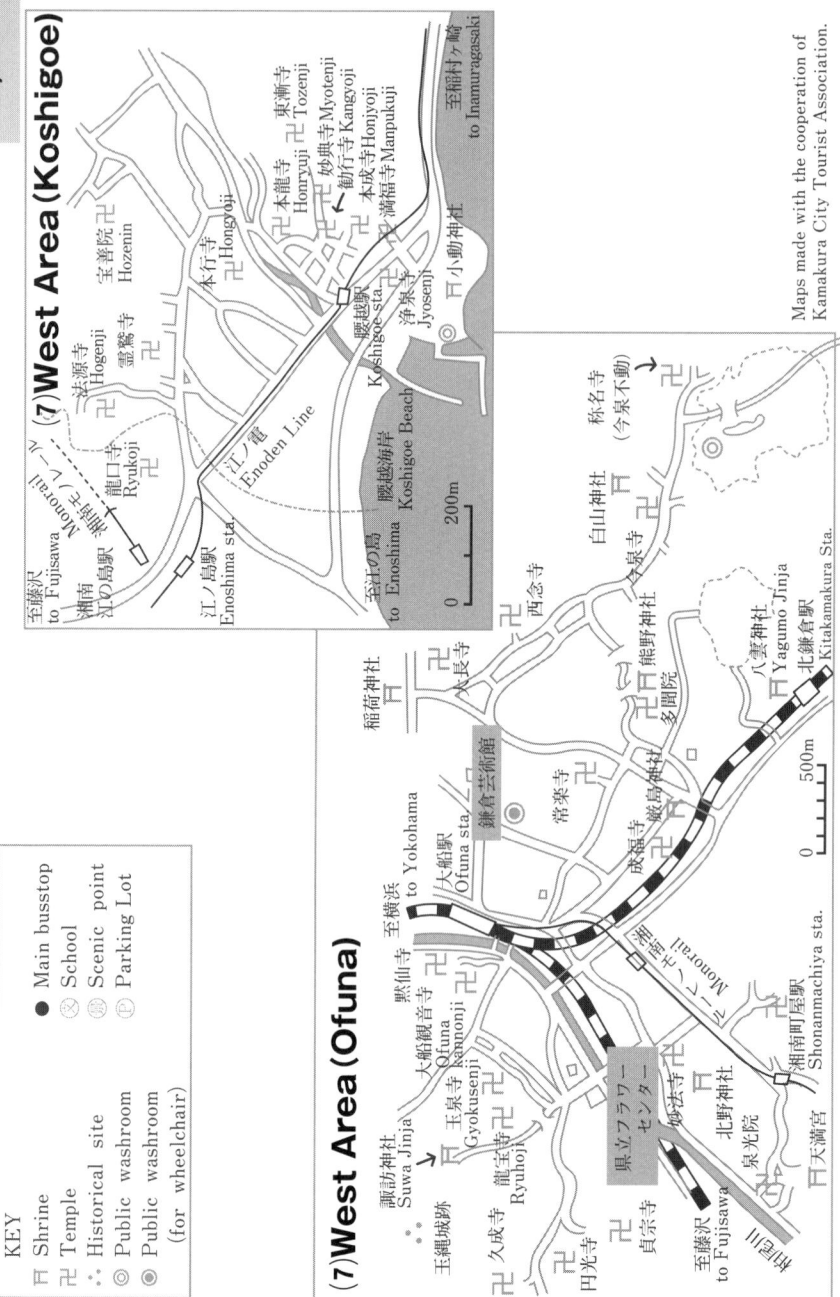

(7) West Area (Koshigoe)

to Fujisawa 至藤沢
湘南江の島駅
江ノ島駅 Enoshima sta.
龍口寺 Ryukoji
Monorail モノレール
腰越駅 Koshigoe sta.
慈源寺 Hogenji
霊鷲寺
宝善院 Hozenin
本行寺 Hongyoji
本龍寺 Honryuji
東漸寺 Tozenji
妙典寺 Myotenji
勧行寺 Kangyoji
本成寺 Honjyoji
満福寺 Manpukuji
浄泉寺 Jyosenji
小動神社
玉江の島 to Enoshima
腰越海岸 Koshigoe Beach
江ノ電 Enoden Line
to Inamuragasaki 至稲村ヶ崎

0 200m

(7) West Area (Ofuna)

to Fujisawa 至藤沢
諏訪神社 Suwa Jinja
玉縄城跡
久成寺
龍宝寺 Ryuhoji
玉泉寺 Gyokusenji
大船観音寺 Ofuna Kannonji
黙仙寺
円光寺
玉光院
貞宗寺
県立フラワーセンター
妙法寺
北野神社
泉光院
天満宮
湘南町屋駅 Shonanmachiya sta.
大船駅 Ofuna sta.
to Yokohama 至横浜
鎌倉芸術館
成福寺
厳島神社
常楽寺
多聞院
稲荷神社
西念寺
白山神社
今泉寺
八雲神社
熊野神社
八幡神社 Yagumo Jinja
北鎌倉駅 Kitakamakura Sta.
称名寺 (今泉不動)
モノレール Monorail

0 500m

KEY
● Main busstop
⊗ School
֍ Scenic point
Ⓟ Parking Lot
卍 Temple
⛩ Shrine
∴ Historical site
◎ Public washroom
◉ Public washroom (for wheelchair)

Maps made with the cooperation of Kamakura City Tourist Association.

An English Guide to Kamakura's Temples & Shrines

by Kenji Kamio and Heather Willson

An English Guide to Kamakura's Temples & Shrines

Map	2
Introduction	13

(1) Central Area
<Nishi-Mikado and Komachi> · 21

Tsurugaoka Hachiman-gu　鶴岡八幡宮	23
Dankazura and Wakamiya-Oji · 27	
Tori-i · 28	
Komainu · 29	
Hokai-ji　宝戒寺	29
10 Famous Wells of Kamakura · 31	
Shirahata Jinja　白幡神社	31
Mysterious Death of Yoritomo · 31	
Yagumo Jinja (Nishimikado)　八雲神社	32
Raiko-ji　来迎寺	33
Daigyo-ji　大巧寺	34
Kamakura-bori (Kamakura Wood-carving) · 36	
Hiruko Jinja　蛭子神社	36
Hongaku-ji　本覚寺	37
Myohon-ji　妙本寺	38
Joei-ji　常栄寺	40
Yagumo Jinja (Omachi)　八雲神社	41
Shinto History · 42	

(2) North Area
<Kita Kamakura> · 45

Engaku-ji　円覚寺	47
Tacchu · 50	
Keisho-an (Engaku-ji Tacchu)　桂昌庵	50
Yabusame · 51	
Fuyo-an (Engaku-ji Tacchu)　富陽庵	51
Densho-an (Engaku-ji Tacchu)　伝宗庵	52
Haku-un-an (Engaku-ji Tacchu)　白雲庵	52
Uncho-an (Engaku-ji Tacchu)　雲頂庵	53
Shorei-in (Engaku-ji Tacchu)　松嶺院	53

Ryoin-an (Engaku-ji Tacchu) 龍隠庵	54
Shozoku-in (Engaku-ji Tacchu) 正続院	55
Sai-in-an (Engaku-ji Tacchu) 済蔭庵	55
Jutoku-an (Engaku-ji Tacchu) 寿徳庵	56
Shoden-an (Engaku-ji Tacchu) 正伝庵	56
Zokuto-an (Engaku-ji Tacchu) 続燈庵	57
Obai-in (Engaku-ji Tacchu) 黄梅院	57
Nyoi-an (Engaku-ji Tacchu) 如意庵	57
Kigen-in (Engaku-ji Tacchu) 帰源院	58
Garyo-an (Engaku-ji Tacchu) 臥龍庵	58

Zen Buddhism and Kamakura · 59

Yagumo Jinja (Yamanouchi) 八雲神社	59
Hachiman Jinja 八幡神社	60
Jofuku-ji 成福寺	61
Joraku-ji 常楽寺	62
Kosho-ji 光照寺	63
Tokei-ji 東慶寺	63
Jochi-ji 浄智寺	64

Kanro-no-i <10 Famous Wells of Kamakura> · 65

Meigetsu-in 明月院	65
Choju-ji (Kencho-ji Tacchu) 長寿寺	66

Kamakura and the Flourishing of Buddhism · 68

Kencho-ji 建長寺	68
Myoko-in (Kencho-ji Tacchu) 妙高院	71
Seirai-an (Kencho-ji Tacchu) 西来庵	71
Dokei-in (Kencho-ji Tacchu) 同契院	72
Hoshu-in (Kencho-ji Tacchu) 宝珠院	72
Ryo-ho-in (Kencho-ji Tacchu) 龍峰院	73
Tengen-in (Kencho-ji Tacchu) 天源院	73
Shoto-in (Kencho-ji Tacchu) 正統院	74
Kaishun-in (Kencho-ji Tacchu) 回春院	74
Zenkyo-in (Kencho-ji Tacchu) 禅居院	75
En-no-ji (Kencho-ji Tacchu) 円応寺	75

(3) North-East Area
<Nikaido and Juniso> · 77

Egara Tenjin-sha 荏柄天神社	79

Ema ・80

Kamakura-gu 鎌倉宮 ... 81
  Omamori・82
  Omikuji ・82

Zuisen-ji 瑞泉寺 ... 83
  Tsurube-no-I <10 Famous Wells of Kamakura> ・84

Kakuon-ji 覚園寺 ... 84
  Munetate-no-I <10 Famous Wells of Kamakura> ・85

Sugimoto-dera 杉本寺 ... 86
  About Kan-non・87

Hokoku-ji 報国寺 ... 87
Jomyo-ji 浄妙寺 ... 88
Kumano Jinja 熊野神社 ... 89
Myo-o-in 明王院 ... 90
Kosoku-ji 光触寺 ... 91
  Roku-Jizo・92

Juniso-Jinja 十二社神社 ... 93

(4) North-West Area
<Sasuke and Ogigayatsu> ・95

Tatsumi Jinja 巽神社 ... 97
Yasaka Daijin 八坂大神 ... 97
Jufuku-ji 寿福寺 ... 98
  Yagura・99

Eisho-ji 英勝寺 ... 100
Kaizo-ji 海蔵寺 ... 102
  Sokonuke-no-i <10 Famous Wells of Kamakura> ・104

Jokomyo-ji 浄光明寺 ... 104
  Izumi-no-i <10 Famous Wells of Kamakura> ・105

Yakuo-ji 薬王寺 ... 106
  Ogi-no-I <10 Famous Wells of Kamakura>・107

Zeniarai Benten Ugafuku Jinja 銭洗弁天宇賀福神社 ... 107
Sasuke Inari Jinja 佐助稲荷神社 ... 108
  Inari Belief・109

Kuzuharaoka Jinja 葛原岡神社 ... 110

(5) South-East Area
<Omachi and Zaimokuza> · 113

Enmei-ji 延命寺	115
Kyo-on-ji 教恩寺	115
Betsugan-ji 別願寺	116
An-yo-in 安養院	117
Jogyo-ji 上行寺	118
Daiho-ji 大宝寺	119
Kiridoshi · 120	
Ankokuron-ji 安国論寺	120
Myoho-ji 妙法寺	121
Chosho-ji 長勝寺	122
What is Shiten-no? · 124	
Choshi-no-i <10 Famous Wells of Kamakura> · 124	
Hossho-ji 法性寺	124
Nichiren and Kamakura · 125	
Moto-hachiman-jinja 元八幡神社	126
Honko-ji 本興寺	127
Tsuji-no-Yakushido · 127	
Keiun-ji 啓運寺	128
Kofuku-ji 向福寺	128
Myocho-ji 妙長寺	129
Jisso-ji 実相寺	130
Raiko-ji (Zaimokuza) 来迎寺	130
Gosho Jinja 五所神社	131
Kuhon-ji 九品寺	132
Fudaraku-ji 補陀洛寺	133
Zaimokuza History · 134	
Komyo-ji 光明寺	134
Senju-in 千手院	137
Renjo-in 蓮乗院	138
Rokkaku-no-I <10 Famous Wells of kamakura> · 138	

(6) South-West Area
<Hase and Gokuraku-ji> · 141

Kotoku-in (Great Buddha) 高徳院	143
Hase-dera 長谷寺	144

Jizo-do · 146
Jizo · 146

Kosoku-ji 光則寺 — 147
Amanawa Shinmei-gu 甘縄神明宮 — 149
Shugen-ji 収玄寺 — 150
Goryo Jinja 御霊神社 — 151
Joju-in 成就院 — 152
Seigetsu-no-i <10 Famous Wells of Kamakura> · 153
Gokuraku-ji 極楽寺 — 153
Legend of Tsukikage Jizo · 156
Kumano Shingu 熊野新宮 — 158
Reiko-ji 霊光寺 — 158

(7) West Area
<Koshigoe and Ofuna> · 161

Josen-ji 浄泉寺 — 163
Koyurugi Jinja 小動神社 — 164
Manpuku-ji 満福寺 — 165
Honjo-ji 本成寺 — 167
Kangyo-ji 勧行寺 — 167
Myoten-ji 妙典寺 — 168
Tozen-ji 東漸寺 — 168
Honryu-ji 本龍寺 — 169
Hozen-in 宝善院 — 169
Hogen-ji 法源寺 — 170
Ryuko-ji 龍口寺 — 171
Joryu-ji 常立寺 — 173
Honren-ji 本蓮寺 — 174
Enoshima Jinja 江島神社 — 175
Ryuko Myojinsha 龍口明神社 — 177
Shoren-ji 青蓮寺 — 178
Ofuna Kan-non-ji 大船観音寺 — 179

Introduction

Kamakura is a city located in Kanagawa Prefecture, Japan, about 50 km south-south-west of Tokyo. The city of Kamakura has an estimated population of 171,241 and area of 39.50km². It is surrounded by mountains on three sides and the open water of Sagami Bay on the fourth. Kamakura has a wide, sandy beach which, in combination with the temples and the proximity to Tokyo, makes it a popular tourist destination. There are more than 170 Buddhist temples and 40 Shinto shrines in the entire area of Kamakura.

The most visited places among them would be the world famous Great Buddha, the many Zen temples, the gorgeous Tsurugaoka Hachiman-gu shrine and the many temples related to the Master Nichiren. They are situated throughout the city, but are not hard to visit in a short time because Kamakura is a small town. You can enjoy a one-day walking trip or use the city bus service, trams or monorail. Also, rent-a-cycle is convenient and enjoyable.

This book is composed of 7 sections:

(1) **Central Area <Nishi-Mikado and Komachi>**
(2) **North Area <Kita Kamakura>**
(3) **North-East Area <Nikaido and Juniso>**
(4) **North-West Area <Sasuke and Ogi-gayatsu>**
(5) **South-East Area <Omachi and Zaimokuza>**
(6) **South-West Area <Hase and Gokuraku-ji>**
(7) **West Area <Koshigoe and Ofuna>**

Every section of this book offers some model courses in order to help visitors plan their trip.

We tried to make a "complete" guide book on Kamakura, but for practical reasons, we had to delete many temples and shrines that are too remote, hard to find or less crucial. However, we still included **96 Buddhist temples** and **23 Shinto shrines** in this guide book.

Unless stated otherwise, the temple or shrine is always open to the public, and admission is free.

Kamakura era

In medieval times, Kamakura was one of the best situated natural fortresses, which allowed the rulers to establish a safe base of their governance for many centuries. During the Heian period, Kamakura was the chief city of Eastern Japan, and from 1192 to 1333, the Minamoto Family ruled Japan from here under what is known as the Kamakura Shogunate. Kamakura became the political center of Japan when Minamoto Yoritomo chose the city as the capital of his new military government in 1192. The Shogunate is called Bakufu in Japanese, which literally means Tent Headquarters (The warrior government set in the battlefield.)

The Kamakura bakufu was not a national regime, however, and although it controlled large tracts of land, there was strong resistance to the stewards. The regime continued warfare against the Fujiwara clan in the north, but never brought either the north nor the west under complete military control.

The old court resided in Kyoto, continuing to hold the land over which it had jurisdiction, while newly organized military families were attracted to Kamakura.

Despite a strong beginning, Yoritomo failed to consolidate the leadership of his family on a lasting basis. Intrafamily contention had long existed within the Minamoto clan, although Yoritomo had eliminated most serious challengers to his authority. When he died suddenly in 1199, his son Minamoto Yoriie became shogun and the nominal head of the Minamoto, but Yoriie was unable to control the other eastern military clans.

By the early thirteenth century, a regency had been established for the shogun by his maternal grandparents, members of the Hojo family, a branch of the Taira that had allied itself with the Minamoto in 1180. Under the Hojo, the Bakufu became powerless, and the shogun, often a member of the Fujiwara family or even an imperial prince, was merely a figurehead.

With the protector of the Emperor a figurehead himself, strains appeared between Kyoto and Kamakura, and in 1221, the Jokyu War broke out between the Cloistered Emperor and the Hojo regent. The Hojo forces easily won the war, and the imperial court was brought under direct bakufu control. The shogun's constables gained greater civil powers, and the court was obliged to seek Kamakura's approval for all of its actions. Although deprived of political power, the court was allowed to retain extensive estates with which to sustain the imperial splendor the bakufu needed to help sanction its rule.

Several significant administrative achievements were made during the Hojo regency. In 1225, the Council of State was established, providing opportunities for other military lords to exercise judicial and legislative authority in Kamakura. The Hojo regent presided over the council, which was a successful form of collective leadership. The adoption of Japan's first military code of law, the Joei

Shikimoku, in 1232, reflected the profound transition from court to militarized society. While legal practices in Kyoto were still based on 500 year old Confucian principles, the Joei Shikimoku code was a highly legalistic document that stressed the duties of stewards and constables, provided means for settling land disputes, and established rules governing inheritances. It was clear and concise, stipulated punishments for violators of its conditions, and remained in effect for the next 635 years.

Muromachi era

To further weaken the Kyoto court, the Bakufu decided to allow two contending imperial line's known as the Southern Court or junior line and the Northern Court or senior line, to alternate on the throne. The method worked for several successions until a member of the Southern Court ascended to the throne as Emperor Godaigo (1318-1339). Godaigo wanted to overthrow the Bakufu, and he openly defied Kamakura by naming his own son his heir.

In 1331, the Bakufu exiled Godaigo, but loyalist forces rebelled. They were aided by Ashikaga Takauji (1305-1358), a constable who turned against Kamakura when dispatched to put down Godaigo's rebellion. At the same time, another eastern chieftain rebelled against the Bakufu, which quickly disintegrated, and the Hojo were defeated.

The Kamakura Shogunate lasted for 130 years, first under the Minamoto shogun and then under the Hojo regents. The Kamakura period ended in 1333 with the destruction of the shogunate and the short re-establishment of the imperial system under Emperor Godaigo by Ashikaga Takauji.

In the swell of victory, Godaigo endeavored to restore imperial authority and tenth-century Confucian practices. This period of reform, known as the Kenmu Restoration (1333 1336), aimed at strengthening the position of the Emperor and reasserting the primacy of the court nobles over the bushi (military clans).

The reality, however, was that the forces who had arisen against Kamakura had been set on defeating the Hojo, not on supporting the Emperor. Ashikaga Takauji finally sided with the Northern Court in a civil war against the Southern Court represented by Godaigo. The long war between the court lasted from 1336 to 1392. Early in the conflict, Godaigo was driven from Kyoto, and the Northern Court contender was installed by Ashikaga, who became the new shogun.

Civil War

The Muromachi Bakufu ended with the unstable political-social situation in

Kyoto around the mid 15th century.

Not only the numerous clans claiming power, but also riots by the farmers who were suffering from drought and famine, weakened the Ashikaga Reign. Kyoto became a city of battles for almost a century.

By that time, Kamakura was under control of the Miura clan. In 1495, Hojo Soun, from another Hojo family, invaded Odawara, and in 1516, beat the Miura clan, kicking them out of Kamakura. Hojo built the invincible Tamanawa castle in Ofuna and conquered the major part of Kanto area. Their power lasted for 100 years.

In 1590, Toyotomi Hideyoshi came to power in western Japan and advanced his army to the east. Then, the already weak Hojo surrendered and Odawara castle and Tamanawa castle were taken over by Tokugawa Ieyasu, then still a top vassal to Hideyoshi.

Hideyoshi established his capital in Osaka in 1590, but died 8 years later. Now came the time of Ieyasu. He gathered forces of various clans to finally defeat the Toyotomi forces in 1600 to start his own 300 year long Tokugawa Shogunate in Edo (Tokyo).

Edo era

Under Ieyasu, Kamakura had a hard time. Ieyasu took care of Tsurugaoka Hachiman-gu because he claimed to be a Minamoto descendant. He also protected and helped financially certain temples such as Tokei-ji, Eisho-ji, Komyo-ji, Engaku-ji and Kencho-ji. However, on the other hand, he charged heavier taxes on the other temples and shrines, which caused a decline in religious activity in Kamakura. As temples fell into ruin, Kamakura turned into just a poor village that made its living by fishing and farming.

Fortunately though, as Kamakura was located near Edo, people began to visit Enoshima, the Great Buddha and Hachiman-gu. Kamakura thus started to be a tourist site in the early 17th century.

Toward the end of the Tokugawa Shogunate in the 19th century, as the menace from the great Western powers increased, numerous coast guard units were posted in Katase, Koshigoe, Yuigahama or Zaimokuza.

After Yokosuka port was opened, many foreigners started to visit Kamakura on holidays. There was even an incident in which a samurai-ronin killed a British army officer at the Geba crossing in 1864.

Meiji Restoration

The modernized Japan brought a significant and unique change to Kamakura. When the Shinbutsu Bunri Seisaku (Shinto and Buddhism Segregation Policy) was issued in 1886, all the Buddhist related objects, buildings and personel were removed from the Shinto shrines and in a similar way, Shinto things were removed from Buddhist temples. It was rather in favor of the Shinto side because Japan's political leaders were very nationalistic and Shinto was the key to implant the Emperor-as-God way of thinking onto the nation.

Simultaneously, a strong movement of rejecting Buddhist influences was everywhere. In Kamakura, they destroyed many temple buildings, burned precious cultural assets and even many statues and objects were stolen. Kamakura lost a great deal of valuable cultural treasures.

Another change came in 1872, when the new Education Law was issued. In Kamakura, ten elementary schools were opened making use of the temples for the class rooms. These temple schools later became the official public schools.

Also, in 1880, a German medical doctor called Erwin Von Beltz publicly introduced Kamakura as a pleasant resort convenient to Tokyo. Thus started the new era of Kamakura's modern image.

As Japan's military force grew, in 1889, the government constructed a railway from Ofuna to Yokosuka, where the military port was located.

Kamakura developed smoothly for the next several decades just like the other cities in the country. However, in 1923, the Great Earthquake that struck all the Kanto region destroyed 70% of houses in Kamakura and killed 412 people. Many temples and shrines collapsed, but within only three years, they succeeded in reconstructing this ancient historical capital.

After the War

During W.W.II, Americans did not bomb Kamakura. It was intentionally saved, along with Kyoto and Nara for cultural reasons.

In the 50s, the city of Kamakura pushed a new housing policy, and the population increased. Various industries were invited to Ofuna and Fukazawa areas. When the citizens became aware of Kamakura's diminishing precious natural environment, they formed the Committee for Environmental Preservation as a watchdog, and in 1966, the Ancient Capital Preservation Law was issued. Since then, no new development can proceed without official permission. Also, in central Kamakura, one cannot construct a building more than four storeys high.

Today, Kamakura's many historical temples and shrines are visited by thousands of people every day. The most famous of these would be Kotoku-in, with the monumental outdoor bronze statue of the Great Buddha. A 15th century tsunami destroyed the temple that once housed the Great Buddha, but the statue stayed firm and has remained outdoors ever since.

Magnificent Zen temples such as Kencho-ji and Engaku-ji, Tokei-ji (a nunnery refuge for women who wanted to divorce their husbands), Tsurugaoka Hachiman-gu Shrine, the ancient Kan-non temple Hase-dera, the graves of Minamoto Yoritomo and Hojo Masako, and Kamakura-gu, where Prince Morinaga was executed, are also listed at the top of Kamakura's most famous historical and religious sites.

Co-existence of Buddhism and Shintoism

The introduction to Japan of writing in the 5th century and Buddhism in the 6th century had a profound impact on the development of a unified system of Shinto beliefs.

Within a brief period of time in the early Nara period, the Kojiki (The Record of Ancient Things, 712) and the Nihon-shoki (The Chronicles of Japan, 720) were written by compiling existing myths and legends into a unified account. These accounts were written with two purposes in mind.

First, was the introduction of Taoist, Confucian, and Buddhist themes into Japanese religion. Second was to shore up support for the legitimacy of the Imperial house, based on its lineage from the Sun Goddess Amaterasu. Much of the area of modern Japan was under only fragmentary control by the Imperial family, and rival ethnic groups (including, perhaps, the ancestors of the Ainu) continued to war against the encroachment of the Japanese. The mythological anthologies, along with other poetry anthologies such as the Man-yoshu, were all meant to impress others with the worthiness of the Imperial family and their divine mandate to rule.

With the introduction of Buddhism and its rapid adoption by the court, it was necessary to explain the apparent differences between native Japanese beliefs and Buddhist teachings.

Indeed, Shinto did not even have a name until it became necessary to distinguish it from Buddhism. One explanation saw the Japanese local gods, kami, as supernatural beings still caught in the cycle of birth and rebirth. The kami are born, live, die, and are reborn like all other beings in the karmic cycle. However, the kami played a special role in protecting Buddhism and allowing its teachings of compassion to flourish.

This explanation was later challenged by Kukai, who saw the kami as different embodiments of the Buddhas themselves. For example, he famously linked Amaterasu, Sun Goddess and ancestor of the Imperial family, with Dainichi Nyorai, a central manifestation of the Buddha, whose name is literally Great Sun Buddha. In his view, the kami were just Buddhas by other names. Buddhism and Shinto coexisted and were amalgamated in the Shinbutsu Shugo, and Kukai's syncretic view held wide sway up until the end of the Edo period.

At that time, there was a renewed interest in Japanese studies (Kokugaku), perhaps as a result of the closed country policy. In the 18th century, various Japanese scholars, in particular Moto-ori Norinaga (1730 1801), tried to tease apart the "real" Shinto from various foreign influences. The attempt was largely unsuccessful since, as early as the Nihon-shoki, parts of the mythology were explicitly borrowed from Chinese doctrines. (For example, the co-creator deities Izanami and Izanagi are explicitly compared to yin and yang.) However, the attempt did set the stage for the arrival of state Shinto following the Meiji Restoration, when Shinto and Buddhism were separated (Shinbutsu bunri).

Nowadays, with the right to religious freedom, most Japanese observe both Shinto and Buddhist rituals at different times of their lives. At New Year's, for example, towards midnight on New Year's Eve, many go to a Buddhist temple to toll the bell and pray, but on New Year's day, they pray to the rising sun and go to a Shinto shrine to make a wish by clapping hands and bowing. They practice two different religious acts within several hours and feel no uneasiness or contradiction at all. Other examples include family events. Most happy events such as weddings and Miya Mairi (Christenings) are at Shinto shrines, but most funerals are at Buddhist temples.

One indigenous belief and one religion originating in India co-exist perfectly together here. How such a thing is possible and why they can practice two different religions at the same time, one domestic and the other imported, are enigmas of Japan.

Visiting temples and shrines

At shrines, besides the tori-i gate and main shrine building, there can be a variety of additional buildings such as the priest's house and office, a storehouse for mikoshi and other auxiliary buildings. Cemeteries, on the other hand, are almost never found at shrines, because death is considered a cause of impurity in Shinto, and in Japan, it is dealt with mostly by Buddhism.

The architecture and features of Shinto shrines and Buddhist temples have melted together over the centuries. There are several construction styles, most of which show Buddhist influences from the Asian mainland. Only a few of today's shrines are considered to be built in a purely Japanese style. Among them are Shinto's most important shrines, Ise Jingu.

At some temples, visitors burn incense (o-senko) in large incense burners. Purchase a bundle, light them, let them burn for a few seconds and then extinguish the flame by waving your hand rather than by blowing it out. Finally, put the incense into the incense burner and fan some smoke towards yourself as the smoke is believed to have healing power. For example, fan some smoke towards your shoulder if you have an injured shoulder.

You should make a small coin offering at the saisen-bako (offering box) in front of the temple. Then fold your hands quietly and bow. In Buddhist temples, we don't pray by clapping hands.

When entering temple buildings, you may be required to take off your shoes. Leave your shoes on the shelves at the entrance or take them with you in plastic bags provided at some temples.

Photography is usually permitted on the temple grounds. It is forbidden indoors at some temples, so watch for signs.

When visiting a shrine, behave calmly and respectfully. You are not supposed to visit a shrine if you are sick, have an open wound or are in mourning because these are considered causes of impurity.

At the purification fountain near the shrine's entrance, fill a ladle with fresh water and rinse both hands. Then transfer some water into your cupped hand, rinse your mouth and spit the water beside the fountain. You are not supposed to transfer the water directly from the ladle into your mouth nor to swallow the water. You will notice that quite a few visitors skip the mouth rinsing part or the purification ritual altogether.

At the offering hall, throw a coin into the offering box, bow deeply twice, clap your hands twice, bow deeply once more and pray for a few seconds. If there is some type of gong, use it before praying in order to get the kami's attention. Photography is usually permitted at shrines.

(1) Central Area

<Nishi-Mikado and Komachi>

MODEL COURSE (A)	MODEL COURSE (B)
JR Kamakura Sta. east exit ↓ 10min. Wakamiya Oji (Dankazura walkway) ↓ Tsurugaoka Hachimangu shrine ↓ 5min. Hokai-ji ↓ 5min. Myoryu-ji ↓ 3min. Daigyo-ji ↓ 3min. Hiruko Jinja shrine ↓ 1min. Hongaku-ji ↓ 3min. Myohon-ji ↓ 5min. Joei-ji ↓ 3min. Yagumo Jinja shrine (all by walking)	JR Kamakura Sta. east exit ↓ 10min. Wakamiya Oji (Dankazura walkway) ↓ Tsurugaoka Hachimangu shrine ↓ 5min. Shirahata Jinja shrine ↓ 8min. Raiko-ji ↓ 10min. Hokai-ji ↓ 5min. Myoryu-ji ↓ 3min. Daigyo-ji ↓ 3min. Hiruko Jinja shrine ↓ 1min. Hongaku-ji ↓ 3min. Myohon-ji ↓ 5min. Joei-ji ↓ 3min. Yagumo Jinja shrine (all by walking)

central

Tsurugaoka Hachiman-gu 鶴岡八幡宮

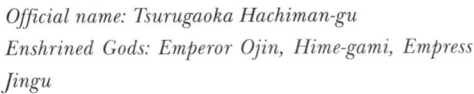

Official name: Tsurugaoka Hachiman-gu
Enshrined Gods: Emperor Ojin, Hime-gami, Empress Jingu
Founded by Minamoto Yoritomo in 1180
Annual festival: September 14-16
Sub shrines: Wakamiya, Takeuchi-sha, Maruyama Inari-sha, Shirahata Jinja, Sorei-sha, Hata-age-sha
Open 9:00-16:00 (Closed on Monday, end of each month)
Admission for Exhibition Hall: ¥100
10 min. from JR Kamakura Sta. east exit
Address: 2-1-31 Yukinoshita, Kamakura City, Kanagawa Pref. Tel: 0467-22-0315

Entrance to the shrine   This is doubtlessly the most visited place in Kamakura. The very origin of this shrine goes back to 1063, when **Minamoto Yoriyoshi**, an ancestor of the Genji family, put a branch shrine of Kyoto's Iwashimizu Hachiman-gu in the Yuigahama area of Kamakura. There, he enshrined the God Hachiman as the guardian spirit of the Minamoto family, and named the shrine Yui Wakamiya or Tsuruoka Wakamiya. This shrine still exists today as Moto (original) Hachiman Jinja in Zaimokuza. Later in 1081, this Yui Wakamiya was restored by **Minamoto Yoshi-ie**, the great-great-grand father of **Minamoto Yoritomo**.

In Japanese medieval history, the Minamoto family (Genji) and the Taira family (Heike), both Bushi or Samurai (warrior) power elites, were sworn foes since the Heiji War of 1159. They fought each other for the actual ruling power of Japan to replace the imperial ruling system. In 1167, Taira-no-Kiyomori came into power by almost entirely wiping out the Minamoto family. However, young Minamoto Yoritomo, one of the few survivors of the Minamoto family, was exiled to Izu, where he succeeded in gathering forces around him over the next ten years. He raised an army and marched into Kamakura to settle his military base in 1180. At this time, he constructed a new shrine at the present site of Tsurugaoka Hachiman-gu, with the dream of defeating the Taira family.

The war between them lasted five years, and finally the Taira armed forces lost the decisive battle in Dan-no-ura in Yamaguchi Pref., leaving Yoritomo as the de facto ruler of Japan.

Nowadays, we consider this shrine purely Shinto, but the truth is considerably different. For almost its whole history until the end of the Edo era in 1868 and the Meiji Restoration, this shrine was practically a temple-shrine. It used to be called Hachiman-gu-ji with its many Buddhist halls such as Yakushi-do, Goma-do, and Nio-mon Gate etc..

Taiko Bashi

To get to Hachiman-gu, go straight east from JR Kamakura station east exit, walk to Wakamiya-Oji at the first traffic lights, turn left and then walk ten minutes to the end of the avenue. It's nicer, of course, to go through the Dankazura walkway that runs in the middle of the avenue. When you see a big vermillion-red Tori-i gate, it is the entrance of Tsurugaoka Hachiman-gu.

To enter the shrine grounds, cross one of the small bridges (there are three small bridges. The one in the middle "Taiko Bashi" (drum bridge) is sharply arched, but nowadays it is usually barred.) Below the bridges is the water of the two ponds on both sides called "Genpei-ike", created in 1182. It is said that Yoritomo's wife, **Hojo Masako**, had the idea of composing two ponds whose landscapes represent the differences between the Minamoto and Taira families. The larger, right-hand pond is the Minamotos' and the smaller is the Tairas'.

Genji-ike pond

white lotus

She planted white (Minamotos' color) lotus flowers in the right pond and red (Tairas' color) lotus in the left pond. Nowadays, however, these differences are gone, and both colors bloom in both ponds during the summer. There are also many tortoises and carp living here. In Buddhism, killing creatures is a sin, and this pond was also made to teach the importance of saving natural life.

On Nakano-shima, one of these three islets, there is a sub-shrine called Hata-age Benzaiten. The goddess worshipped here is originally a Hindu goddess of rivers and music. Once introduced to Japan, she blended with Buddhism and Shintoism over time, and became the Goddess of Water, Fortune, Art and Learning.

Unfortunately, she was regarded as impure

Hata-age Benzaiten Shrine

for a Shinto deity by the Meiji Government and was removed. The present shrine was rebuilt in 1956, and was named Hata-age (flag raising) Benzai-ten after Yoritomo's army which was raised in 1180. Many white banners waving along the approach have been donated by ambitious devotees praying for success in business.

The annual festival for this particular sub-temple is held on the first Serpent Day of April in the lunar calendar.

From the bridges, walk straight along the wide approach, and you will see a vermillion painted, copper roofed stage in the center of the big courtyard. This is the "Maiden", Ritual Dance Stage, which commemorates Lady **Shizuka Gozen**, second wife of **Minamoto Yoshitsune**, the tragic hero of Minamoto history. While Yoshitsune was fleeing, Lady Shizuka was captured in Kyoto, and brought to Kamakura. She was an excellent dancer of Shira-Byoshi (dance in white costume) and on Shogun Yoritomo's orders, Shizuka reluctantly danced in front of Yoritomo.

On the stage, she sang a song expressing her deep feeling toward her beloved fugitive Yoshitsune, which made Yoritomo feel uncomfortable. At the time, Lady Shizuka was pregnant with Yoshitsune's child. Yoritomo ordered it to be killed if it was a boy, which it was. The new born baby boy was killed and thrown into the sea at Yuigahama beach.

Today, dedicatory dances and music are performed on the second Sunday of April every year during the Kamakura Festival in April.

Ascending 60 stone steps, one reaches the shrine's main hall. On the left-hand side of the stone steps stands a 30.5 meter high, more than 1,000 year old gingko tree, called "Kakure Icho". (Kakure means to hide.)

On a snowy January 27, 1219, around 6 o'clock in the evening, on these stone steps, **Minamoto Sanetomo**, the 3rd Shogun and the second son of Yoritomo, was assasinated by his 20 year old nephew, **Minamoto Kugyo**, who was then chief administrater of the shrine. He hid behind the tree and cut Sanetomo's head off with a sword when he came out of the Main Hall where they had been having a banquet.

Kakure Icho

Historians don't know exactly why Kugyo had to kill

Honden (Main Hall)

his uncle. Probably he mistakenly thought that Sanetomo had killed his father, or it might have been a set-up by the head of the Hojo family, which was practically running the Government, to eliminate the Minamoto family line. Thereafter, the real power of the Kamakura shogunate did, in fact, fall into the hands of the Hojos'.

In general, a Shinto shrine is composed of the front and back parts. The former is an oratory hall called Haiden, where various kinds of ritual ceremonies and worship are held. The latter is the sanctum, where a sacred metallic mirror, called "Yata-no-Kagami", is enshrined in the altar.

Hachiman-gu enshrines the 15th **Emperor Ojin**, Hime-gami, and **Empress Jingu.** The Minamoto family claimed that they were the descendants of the 56th **Emperor Seiwa (850-880)**, and the Emperor's tutelary deity was the god Hachiman, which is why Yoritomo enshrined Hachiman when he first came into power. The shrine burnt down in 1191, but Yoritomo immediately had it reconstructed. It was also rebuilt in 1828 by **Tokugawa Ienari**, the 11th Tokugawa Shogun. (The Tokugawa family claimed they were descended from the Minamotos, and thus protected the shrine). The style of architecture is called Gongen Zukuri. This consists of two structures, or two gable-roofs in tiers, the oratory in front and the sanctum at the rear, which convey an extraordinary sense of majesty and power.

Wakamiya sub-shrine

To the east of the 61 stone-steps leading to the Main Hall is a smaller sub-shrine called Wakamiya, which is dedicated to **Emperor Nintoku (?-399)**, who was the son of Emperor Ojin. Both were legendary emperors in the latter half of the 4th century. The shrine also worships the **Emperor Richu**, Nakanohime-no-Mikoto and Iwanohime-no-Mikoto.

Reconstruction of the structure was initiated by **Tokugawa Hidetada (1579-1632)**, the 2nd Tokugawa Shogun, and was completed in 1624 while **Tokugawa Iemitsu (1604-1651)** was the 3rd Shogun. The architecture is called Gongen Zukuri, the same as that of the Main Hall. It is constructed on the ground where Yoritomo built the Main shrine for the first time.

Botan-en (Peony garden)

The Peony Garden (Botan-en) was opened in 1980 in commemoration of the shrine's 800th anniversary. The 10,000 square-meter garden skirts along the south-east side of the Genji pond. It boasts of being the biggest flower garden of this kind in the country, containing 200 species. 2,000 peonies bloom from mid-April to late May and the 500 winter peonies, a rarity in Japan, flourish from early January for about a month. Admission fee is necessary.

Treasure Museum (Homotu-den)

The Treasure Museum, where the Shrine's valuable objects are exhibited, is on the left-hand side of the Main Hall. It exhibits seven portable-shrines made in the 17th to 18th centuries, ancient swords, two seated statues of Yoritomo, a folding screen on which battle field scenes between the Minamoto and Taira clans are painted, a twelve-layered robe for court ladies, a suit of armor, ancient brush-caligraphy, and various wooden masks. A notable artifact is a lacquered inkstone case decorated with laminae of mother-of-pearl depicting chrysanthemum flowers with flying birds. The case was granted to Yoritomo by **Emperor Go-Shirakawa**. A gold lacquered arrow case of mother-of-pearl work and black-lacquered arrows are exquisite pieces.

Dankazura and Wakamiya-Oji

The straight broad way between Yuigahama beach and Tsurugaoka Hachiman-gu Shrine, was opened on March 15,1182, by **Minamoto Yoritomo**, the first Shogun of Kamakura, as the approach to the shrine.

Dankazura was originally constructed in 1182 at the command of Yoritomo for his wife, **Hojo Masako**'s safe delivery of their baby. At the age of 36, Yoritomo had two daughters but no heir apparent (a son) to succeed the throne. However, their wish came true the same year. The new baby was a boy, **Yori-ie**, who later assumed the seat as the Second Shogun. The wide road with Dankazura in the center was thus called "Wakamiya-Oji" (Young Prince Avenue).

The broad way was designed like "Suzaku-Oji" broadway in Kyoto, because the shrine worships the same spirit of Iwashimizu Hachiman-gu Shrine in Kyoto. At the occasion of the construction, Shogun Yoritomo himself directed the work and his father-in-law, **Hojo Tokimasa**, together with his men joined the construction laborers.

"Dan" means elavated, and "Kazura" means stone wall (in this case about half a meter high).

Dankazura has a secret in its design. At the beginning, the path measures 4.75m wide, but at the end only 2.5m. One can assume that this design was for the visual effect of making Dankazura's perspective longer, and also the dignity of the shrine became larger than life.

Originally, Wakamiya-Oji ran all the way from the beach to the shrine, but was partly destroyed because of a flood toward the end of the 15th century, and was further cut by the National Railroad construction in the Meiji era.

A recent excavation has revealed that the original avenue was 33 meters wide and had large ditches on both sides (3 meters wide and 1.5 meters deep). The promenade used to stretch from the first tori-i near the beach up to the third one, a distance of 1,500 meters. The perpendicular streets were constructed in such a way that they had to make at least one turning in order to cross the avenue, thus making the city center harder to attack.

In early April, the path becomes a long tunnel of cherry blossoms. The trees, which grew from seedlings planted in 1918, are lit up by strings of lanterns sponsored by local merchants and companies. Dankazura is popular year-round, but is most crowded in early April and on the first days of New Years.

Wakamiya-Oji is one of the most popular downtown streets, together with Komachi-dori which runs parallel a block to the west. On both sides of the avenue, there are shops, restaurants, and hotels.

Tori-i

Ichi-no-Tori-i

Ni-no-Tori-i

At the lower end of Dankazura stands a large, 6m high red Gate. This is a "tori-i", which every Shinto shrine has at its entrance. A Shinto shrine has a courtyard but no gate that can be locked, and is thus always open. We usually can find two stone statues of dogs, another symbol of Shinto shrines, sitting near the gate.

Tsurugaoka Hachiman-gu has three tori-i gates along Wakamiya-Oji.

The first one, Ichi-no-Tori-I, is located further south facing the beach. It was destroyed in the earthquake of 1923 and was reconstructed in 1936 with Mikage (granite) stones from Izu Penisula, which were also used in the original. The second one is the one at the beginning of Dankazura. The third tori-i stands at the Shrine's entrance.

In 2002, an excavation discovered half rotten wooden base piles halfway between Geba crossing and the first tori-i. This is called "Hama-no-tori-i" (Beach Tori-i), which assumingly was built in the Edo era. The wooden piles had been made by using a sort of mosaic technique in order to make it perfectly straight and round.

Komainu

Literally, "Korean dog", these are paired statues of figurative lion-like dog tutelaries found at the entryway to shrine buildings, or alongside their tori-i or approachways. The paired figures are typically male and female, and some are portrayed with horns. In general, the pairs include one with an open mouth and one with its mouth closed, the so-called a-un posture symbolizing the "Yin" and "Yang" of Chinese Taoism.

The word Koma is an ancient term for the Korean peninsula, but since the images were merely transmitted through the Korean peninsula, it may be that the term Komainu was merely used to indicate the "foreign" nature of the figures.

Another style was introduced to Japan from Tong Dynasty China during the Heian period and later from Song China during the Kamakura period, and this style is frequently referred to as Kara-jishi (Chinese lion). "Kara" is the Japanese way of reading the Chinese letter "tong", which means Tong Dynasty. By that period, the most representative foreign country and culture was the Tong of China. China of any dynasty would be Tong for the Japanese, so everything from China was "Kara-something".

Imaginery lions in paintings and sculptures were also introduced to Japan, and especially during the Kamakura period, Chinese culture was a "must" to learn for intellectuals and monks. It is curious that in Shinto, which is of purely Japanese origin, its shrines are always designed with these imported figures of imaginery lion-dogs flanking the main hall.

Hokai-ji 宝戒寺

Official name: Kinryu-zan Shakuman-In Endon Hokai-ji
Sect: Tendai-Shu
Inaugurated by Enkan Echin Ji-i in 1335
Built by Emperor Godaigo
Principal icon (Hon-zon): Kosodate Kyo-yomi Jizo Dai-bosatsu
Open 8:30-16:30
Entrance fee: ¥100
15 min. from JR Kamakura Sta. east exit
Address: 3-5-22 Komachi, Kamakura City, Kanagawa Pref. Tel: 0467-22-5512

Taishi-do

Just one block to the east of the main gate of Tsurugaoka Hachiman-gu Shrine, at the corner of the street, Hokai-ji welcomes visitors with its octagonal shaped stone path. Even though the temple is close to a busy road, once you enter the grounds, the calm and quiet atmosphere envelopes you.

In the Hondo (main temple), on both sides of the altar are spaces where the "Goma" worshipping ceremony is held on the 24th of every month from 13:30. The monks chant sutras around the fire in the center of the hall, burning wood sticks, "Gomaboku" (goma wood sticks) on which people's wishes are written.

The temple was built on the land where the Hojo family's residence used to be. The 14th Shogun of the Hojo Reign, **Hojo Takatoki**, was attacked by **Nitta Yoshisada**'s army in 1333 and he evacuated to another temple called Tosho-ji in the hills behind his home. However, the enemy set fire to Tosho-ji temple and all 870 warriors killed themselves, thus ending the 140 years of the Kamakura Shogunate.

There is no remaining trace of Tosho-ji now, but close to the temple's site, we can visit "Takatoki Yagura" (grave in a grotto), a monument to Takatoki's death.

Kosodate Kyo-yomi Jizo Dai-bosatsu, the Hon-zon of Hokai-ji, standing in the center of the Hon-do, was made in 1365 by Buddhist sculptor Sanjo-Hoin-Ken-en from Kyoto. On either side of the Jizo-Bosatsu, there are two Gods, called Bonten and Taishakuten, who were originally Hindu Gods. This type of composition is quite frequent in Japanese temples.

On the right hand side of the Hon-do, a glowing black Enma Dai-o shows its scary golden teeth in its gaping mouth. Enma Dai-o is the infernal guardian-judge God who decides the final destination of the dead, to heaven or to hell. On the transoms of both sides, beautiful picures of heavenly maidens are hung.

Hokai-ji is famous for its white hagi flowers which bloom throughout the garden in autumn, so it is otherwise called "Hagi no Tera" (temple of bush clovers). We can also enjoy cherry blossoms in spring, 108 different species of camelia from October to May, and Ume (Japanese apricot) in early spring.

Approach way

10 Famous Wells of Kamakura

Kamakura did not have a rich supply of fresh water, so wells of good quality water were a precious resource. Every one of these 10 wells spread all over Kamakura, has its own reason for its fame.

Kurogane-no-i

The "Kurogane-no-i" well is on the corner at the very end of Komachi-dori street. Kurogane means iron. In old times, an iron head of Kan-non was found in the bottom of this well. It was moved to Shi-Kyomizu-dera temple in Hase, but after fire destroyed the Hase area, the Kan-non head was moved to Dai-Kan-non-ji Temple in Ningyo-cho in Tokyo.

Shirahata Jinja　白幡神社

Official name: Shirahata Jinja
Enshrined object: Grave of Minamoto Yoritomo
Distinctive Property: Good luck in competition
Founded in 1189
Annual festival: January 13
15 min. from JR Kamakura Sta. east exit
Annual event: January 13.
Address: 2-1-24 Nishi-mikado, Kamakura City, Kanagawa Pref.

Originally, this was the site of a temple called Hokke-do, built by **Minamoto Yoritomo** and in which he was buried. For centuries, it was greatly respected as one of the most important temples in Kamakura. However, at the Meiji Restoration, Hokke-do temple was demolished and replaced by a Shintoist shrine called Shirahata Jinja. Shirahata means a "White Flag", white being the color of the Minamoto Army. There are many shrines called Shirahata Jinja in Japan, all of which are consecrated to the spirit of the Minamoto family. On the hill behind stands the tomb of Minamoto Yoritomo.

Mysterious Death of Yoritomo

The mystery of Yoritomo's death starts from the historically proven fact that he fell sick on his way back from a ritual ceremony on the Sagami Bridge. The historical record, "Azuma Kagami", says he

Tomb of Minamoto Yoritomo

was seriously injured by a fall from his horse, and this theory is the most generally accepted one. However, it is hard to accept that such an experienced warrior could make such a slip, so some theories add diabetes, a stroke or superstitious shock as possible causes of his sudden death.

It seems that he was suffering from chronic "thirst", which might be a symptom of diabetes. There are many key words concerned with "water" surrounding his death, such as "thirsty", "bridge", or "ghost of drowned Emperor Antoku whom he killed in the war" etc. These all suggest he died because of some trouble with water.

Also, his horse suddenly went wild in river water and might have thrown its rider off into the water... In those ancient times, people were still superstitious, and Yoritomo would not be an exception. The strongly religious Yoritomo might have had nightmares about his younger brother, **Yoshitsune,** or **Emperor Antoku**, both of whom he had mercilessly killed. Or, he might have been assassinated by an avenger, and the fact kept secret for political stability. Some hypothesize that he was mistakenly killed when he was sneaking to his mistress's place in the night.

However, a man like him in the highest position would not need to act so secretly, unless his wife, **Masako**, controlled his night-time activities.

Yagumo Jinja (Nishimikado) 八雲神社

Official name: Yagumo Jinja
Enshrined Gods: Susano-no-mikoto
Founded by Minamoto Yoshimitsu circa 1082
15 min. from JR Kamakura Sta. east exit
Annual festival: July 6.
Sub shrine: Inari Jinja
Address: 1-13-1 Nishi-mikado, Kamakura City, Kanagawa Pref. Tel: 0467-22-3347

This is a Chinju shrine in the Nishi-Mikado area. "Chinju" (or Ujigami) means a local shrine protecting a community or village, where ritual ceremonies or religious events were (or still are) held by community members. However, little is known about this shrine's history, except the records show that the main hall was built in 1832.

There is also a description in the old historical chronicle "Sagami Fudoki" which suggests that a certain shrine called "Tenno-sha of Azadaimon" was originally built here.

Raiko-ji 来迎寺

Official name: Manko-zan Raiko-ji
Sect: Ji-Shu
Built in 1293
Opened by Ikko
Principal icon (Hon-zon): Amida Nyorai
Open 10:00-16:00
Entrance fee: ¥200
Take a bus bound for Kanazawa Hakkei (No.24) or Tachiarai (No.23) from JR Kamakura Sta. east exit. It's a 10 min. walk from Daigaku-mae bus stop or Wakare-michi bus stop.
Address: 1-11-1 Nishimikado, Kamakura City, Kanagawa Pref. Tel: 0467-24-3476

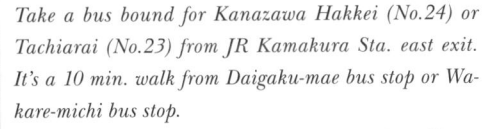

This rather small temple of Ji-Shu denomination is situated near **Minamoto Yoritomo**'s tomb. There are only six Ji-Shu temples in Kamakura, and two of them are called Raiko-ji, one in Zaimokuza area and the other here in Nishimikado area, just behind Tsurugaoka Hachiman-gu shrine.

Ji-shu was derived from Jodo-Shu sect. It was established by the Master **Ippen**, who opened Yugyo-ji Temple in Fujisawa.

In the Hon-do, Amida Nyorai statue (the main icon of the temple) is posed with Nyoirin Kan-non on its right hand side and Jizo Bosatsu on its left. The Hon-zon was made in 1712 (Edo era) and the Jizo Bosatsu in 1384.

Nyoirin Kan-non has a very similar feature to the Hon-zon of Jokomyo-ji, Amida Sanzon. Song Dynasty style of decorative sculpture can be observed, such as the slightly inclining face, the crown on the head, or the hands, and fingers, posture. The patterns on the clothings, called "Domon", is a very typical icon carving technique of Kamakura region in that period. This Nyoirin Kan-non is yet today strongly worshipped for safe delivery.

The Jizo Bosatsu is unusually posed like a Zen meditator, with his clothing draped loosely over the pedestal. On his left, a curious figure of a monk holding a bamboo cane is Zen-shu master Baddabara, who is believed to cure headaches, hip pain and eye diseases.

Myoryu-ji 妙隆寺

Official name: Eisho-zan Myoryu-ji
Sect: Nichiren-Shu
Inaugurated by Nichiei
Built by Chiba Tsunetane in 1385
Principal icon (Hon-zon): Shakamuni-Butsu
12 min. from JR Kamakura Sta. east exit
Address: 2-17-20 Komachi, Kamakura City, Kanagawa Pref. Tel: 0467-23-3195

Master Nisshin

This temple is situated on Komachi-Oji street, one block east of Wakamiya-Oji, not far from Daigyo-ji. The founder, **Chiba Tsunetane**, was one of the powerful followers of the Kamakura Shogunate and used to reign over Chiba province. Tsunetane founded Myoryu-ji to worship his ancestors, and established **Nichiei** of Nakayama Hokke-ji temple (in Chiba Pref.) as the temple master.

The 2nd chief priest, **Nisshin**, was a very disciplined monk. He appealed to Shogun Ashikaga Yoshimasa to follow his advice according to his political-religious thesis "Rissho-chikoku-ron". This made the Shogun angry, who then had Nisshin arrested and tortured by placing a burning pan on his head. However, he stubbornly stuck to his opinion, so the Shogun finally released him. Since then, he has otherwise been called "Nabekamuri Nisshin" (Pan hat Nisshin).

On the right hand side of the Hon-do, a basin he used to practice austerities with is preserved and a stone statue of him is posed in the Nisshin-do in the back.

Daigyo-ji 大巧寺

Official name: Chokei-zan Shogaku-in Daigyo-ji
Sect: Nichiren-Shu
Built by Niccho in 1532
Principal icon (Hon-zon): Onme Reijin
Open 9:00-17:00
3 min. from JR Kamakura Sta. west exit
Address: 1-9-28 Komachi, Kamakura City, Kanagawa

Pref. Tel: 0467-22-0639

Main gate

To get to the nearest temple to Kamakura station, walk straight east from the station, crossing the main Wakamiya-Oji Avenue, and you will see a gate with a red rock monument in front. This is the entrance to Daigyo-ji, otherwise called "Onme-sama", the God of safe delivery. Here is the legend of the temple.

In an early morning in 1536, **Nitto**, the priest of the temple, was on the way to Myohon-ji temple to worship. When he was going to cross the Namerikawa river (a tiny river that crosses Kamakura from east to south-west), he found a woman crying in pain on the river bed. Her hair was ruffled and she was dressed in bloodstained clothing. She was holding a skinny baby in her arms. Nitto asked her, "What's the matter with you, lady? Why are you crying in such a place?"

"I am the wife of Akiyama Kageyu in Okura. I died a few days ago because of a difficult delivery. I have been trying to cross this river to go to the other side for several days, but, as the water is dirty with blood, I can't see how deep it is. In addition, my baby desperately sucks at my breast, so I am in pain. Please help me."

It was the dead woman's spirit who was lost on the way to heaven.

Nitto then told her to believe in Buddha and chant the sutra to remove the pain. He himself started to chant the sutra, and when he opened his eyes, the woman was gone.

Some days later, a beautiful woman visited him and expressed her gratitude.

"Thanks to you, my pain has gone. I brought all the money I saved in my life time. Please use it to build a cenotaph for suffering pregnant women."

Ceiling reliefs

Nitto went to see her husband Akiyama Kageyu and explained had what happened. Akiyama recognized the package of money. It was his deceased wife's.

Soon after, Nitto built a stone tower and dedicated it to the God of safe delivery, called "Ubume Reijin". This "Ubume" turned "into Unme" or "Onme" as time went on.

The approach to the main temple (Hon-den) is paved in stone and lightly meanders between richly planted garden beds. There are always mothers and families

35

here, praying for their safe delivery or giving thanks for their new born babies.

The ceiling of the Hon-den is segmented into many square frames that are decorated with colorful reliefs of bird and animal figures. The temple is relatively small but has a very gentle feeling.

Kamakura-bori (Kamakura Wood-carving)

Kamakura-bori is a multi-layer lacquered wood-carving handicraft produced in Kamakura. It dates all the way back to the 13th century when there were excellent sculptors in Kamakura who carved Buddhist statues. In the neighborhood of Jufuku-ji Temple especially, there lived many sculptors of Buddhist statues, such as the Goto, Mitsuhashi and Kano families. They contributed to the development of wood-carving techniques, and many of the statues made during the Kamakura period were carved by members of those families. Their technique was passed on from one generation to the next. As the years progressed and culture in Kamakura declined, however, Buddhist statues were no longer in demand. They gradually switched from carving Buddhist statues to utensils such as trays used in the home, using the technique they inherited from their ancestors. This eventually produced today's Kamakura lacquered wood-carving called Kamakura-Bori.

Kamakura Wood-Carving Hall, established in 1968, is located on Wakamiya-Oji street near Hongaku-ji and its ground floor showroom for new products is open to the public.

Hiruko Jinja　蛭子神社

Official name: Hiruko Jinja
Enshrined Gods: Onamuchi-no-Mikoto
Distinctive property: Happiness, family safety, business prosperity
Annual festival: Closest Sunday to August 15
5 min. from JR Kamakura Sta. east exit
Address: 2-23-3 Komachi, Kamakura City, Kanagawa Pref.

This local shrine in the Komachi area was originally a shrine called Ebisu Saburo-sha near Ebisu-bashi bridge in front of Hongaku-ji temple. Between 1429-1441, when Hongaku-ji was first built, the shrine was moved into the temple's courtyard.

However, in the Meiji Restoration, the segregation of Buddhism and Shintoism forced the shrine to be moved back to its original (present) location in 1874. They used the Imamiya Shrine building, which was then in Tsurugaoka Hachiman-gu, as the new Hiruko Jinja Shrine building. At this time, the name Ebisu was changed to Hiruko, which has the same meaning. Hiruko in kanji can be read "Ebisu", which means "stranger", "devil", "drowned body", or "sea mammal such as dolphin, whale or shark".

Hongaku-ji 本覚寺

Official name: Myogon-zan Hongaku-ji
Sect: Nichiren-Shu
Built by Nisshutsu in 1436
Principal icon: Shaka Sanzon
3 min. from JR Kamakura Sta. east exit
Address: 4-4-18 Komachi, Kamakura City, Kanagawa Pref. Tel: 0467-22-0490

After Daigyo-ji, Hongaku-ji is the second closest temple to Kamakura station. For the easiest access, cross Wakamiya-Oji Ave., turn left at the corner past the post office, and after a few minutes walk, you will find the temple's north gate on the right hand side of the street. As its main gate faces Komachi-Oji street on the far side, the temple grounds are used as a short cut by the local residents.

Hongaku-ji is famous as a place to worship the God Ebisu. Ebisu or Ebisu-sama is a very popular God, and is said to protect life and wealth. Ebisu is one of the seven Gods of happiness, or "Shichi-Fuku-Jin".

Originally, this was the site of an Ebisu temple of the Tendai-shu denomination, which was built by **Minamoto Yoritomo** to worship the Guardian God during his Kamakura reign. When **Nichiren** returned to Kamakura from Sado Island, where he had been exiled, he preached here in the Ebisu temple for the last time before leaving for Minobu Mountain where he was to build a new temple.

60 years later, when the Kamakura reign collapsed, Ebisu temple was burnt down. 160 years later, a monk called **Nisshutsu (1380-1459)** of Nichiren-shu showed up in Kamakura to do his missionary work. Like his master Nichiren had been during the Kamakura reign, Nisshutsu was

Ebisu-do hall

37

severely oppressed by the governor, **Ashikaga Mochiuji**. However, the morale and the solidarity of his followers were so strong that Governor Mochiuji was moved and overturned his oppressive policy, and eventually asked Nisshutsu to build a new temple on the land where Ebisu temple used to be.

In 1436, Nisshutsu changed the temple to Nichiren-shu, respectfully keeping up the enshrinement of Ebisu. Later, his successor **Niccho** (1421-1500, 11th head priest of the Minobu temple) would bring the ashes of Nichiren here from Minobu-san Kuon-ji Temple (the head temple of Nichiren-shu denomination. This made it easier for the physically weakened and old to visit Nichiren's remains without having to make the long pilgrimage to Nichiren's final resting place in the mountains. The Shari-den built next to the Hondo is where Nichiren's ashes have been kept ever since.

Hongaku-ji is also popular for its magical curing of eye diseases. "Niccho-sama" is the legend of the magic spell which saved a 61 year old man's eyesight in 1482. Master Niccho suffered from eye disease and had almost lost his sight, but after chanting the Hokke-kyo sutra, he recovered without the aid of a doctor.

In the cemetry is the tomb of **Masamune**, the legendary great Katana (Japanese sword) maker. Masamune was a son of sword maker, who improved the various defects of Japanese swords that came to light during the two battles against Mongolian invaders in western Japan. He changed the form of the point, hardened the steel, made the sword thinner to cut sharper and succeeded in making a heavyduty sword of flexible quality by combining hard and soft parts of steel. It is said his swords were able to cut through armor and helmets made of iron.

Sword maker Masamune's tomb

Myohon-ji 妙本寺

Official name: Choko-zan Myohon-ji
Sect: Nichiren-Shu
Inaugurated by Nichiren in 1260
Built by Hiki Daigaku Saburo Yoshimoto
Principal icon: Jukkai Daimandara Gohonzon
Entrance fee (as offering): ¥100, residents and students free
8 min. from JR Kamakura Sta. east exit

San-mon

Address: 1-15-1 Omachi, Kamakura City, Kanagawa Pref. Tel: 0467-22-0777

From the gate of Hongaku-ji, turn left after crossing the small Ebisu-do bridge, and one finds the entrance gate of Myohon-ji at the far end of the road. To reach its Sanmon, or main gate, one walks some 100 meters up a long slope. Although Myohon-ji is situated less than 10 minutes walk from the station, as one goes up the slope, the scenery changes to that of a deep mountain valley, and complete tranquility takes visitors to another world.

The Sanmon is called Niten-mon. Niten means two of four Guardian Gods "Shiten-no". Here we find Jikoku-ten and Tamon-ten. The huge building in front, "Soshi-do," nestled in the forested hills, is where the statue of Nichiren is kept.

The temple was built by **Hiki Yoshimoto** on his own residential land.

On the right hand side of the garden, along the cliff-like wall, we find tombs of all the Hiki family members and their relatives. These tombs previously were in Ankokuron-ji, but were moved in the 1920's to Myohon-ji.

Myohon-ji holds a sad story of the extermination of the Hiki family, which was caused by power succession troubles within the Hojo family.

In 1199, **Minamoto Yoritomo** suddenly died. His eldest son, **Yori-ie**, succeeded the Shogunate and became the second Kamakura Shogun at the age of 18. However, in realty, the controlling power was not in his own hands, but in his grandfather, **Hojo Tokimasa**'s, and his mother's, now the widow **Masako**. Yori-ie married **Wakasa**, the daughter of **Hiki Yoshikazu**, whose aunt had been the nurse of former Shogun Yoritomo. The 2nd Kamakura Shogun relied heavily on his father-in-law, Hiki Yoshikazu.

Nichiren

This did not please his grandfather, Hojo Tokimasa. Soon, Wakasa gave birth to a child, **Kazuhata**. This new born baby boy should have been the next successor, but Hojo Tokimasa, who took his own power for granted, started to feel uneasy by the tight and growing relationship between Minamoto and Hiki. Tokimasa had to get rid of the Hiki family, and persuaded his daughter, Masako, to make a move in order to replace the Shogun with her son, Sanetomo, who was nine years younger than Yori-ie. Hiki noticed this con-

Tomb of the Hiki Family

Jakushi-do

spiracy, became watchful, and even planned to counter-attack Hojo. Meanwhile Tokimasa subtly approached Hiki and invited him to peace talks at his residence, where he assassinated him. Hojos' men subsequently attacked Hiki's residence and the house was burnt to ashes, killing the Shogun's wife, Wakasa, and his son Kazuhata who was only 6 years old.

In 1203, Sanetomo succeeded as the 3rd Shogun at 11 years of age, but of course, being so young, had no real power. Yori-ie was exciled by Hojo to Izu and was finally assassinated in 1204 at the young age of 23.

Myohon-ji founder **Hiki Yoshimoto** was the only surviver of this misfortune. He fled to Kyoto, met Nichiren and became his disciple. Yoshimoto returned to Kamakura at an old age to build a temple to mourn his ancestors on the family's property.

After the death of the Shogun's wife, Wakasa, and his 6 years old son Kazuhata, the daughter of **Hojo Masamura** became seriously ill. She acted haunted, talked deliriusly and crawled like a snake apparently under the influence of the spirit of the murdered Wakasa. Masamura therefore built a hall of worship, Jakushi-do, for her. Eventually, his daughter recovered. Jakushi-do is situated deep in the hill on the left hand side where the approach way begins.

Joei-ji 常栄寺

Official name: Eun-zan Joei-ji
Sect: Nichiren-Shu
Inaugurated by Nissho in 1606
Built by Nichiyu Honi
Principal icon: Sanbo Soshi
Open 9:00-17:00
8 min. from JR Kamakura Sta. east exit
Address: 1-12-11 Zaimokuza, Kamakura City, Kanagawa Pref. Tel: 0467-22-4570

To get to this temple, go into the street on the right hand side of the outer gate of Myohon-ji temple and keep on walking for some minutes.

Small but famous for its popular name "Botamochi-dera" (Botamochi or Mochi means rice cake), it also has to do with **Nichiren**.

Myo-Jo-Nichi-Ei offering Mochi to Nichiren

On September 12 in 1271, Nichiren was arrested by Kamakura Shogun **Hojo Tokimune** and sentenced to death. When he was pilloried around on horse back before being taken to Enoshima to be executed, a woman courageously stepped out from the bystanding crowd in the street and offered him a package of rice cake. The woman who proferred the rice cake later became a nun called **Myo-Jo-Nichi-Ei**.

The temple was built on the place where she lived, and was named after her. Every year on September 12, people celebrate the day Nichiren survived, offering rice cakes to his icon and also to visitors. The very place where the "suspended execution" happened is in Ryuko-ji in Koshigoe, near Enoshima Station on the Enoden tramway (20 min. from Kamakura, see West Kamakura section).

Yagumo Jinja (Omachi) 八雲神社

Official name: Yagumo Jinja
Enshrined Gods: Susano-no-Mikoto, Inadanohime-no-Mikoto, Hachioji-no-Mikoto, Spirits of Satake Family
Founded by Shiragi-no-Saburo Yoshimitsu in 1081-1084
Distinctive property: Good luck and protection from all disasters and evil.
Annual festival: 3 days between July 7-14 over a weekend
Sub shrines: Mitake Sanpo-sha, Inari Jinja, Suwa Jinja and Oiwa Inari-sha
8 min. from JR Kamakura Sta. east exit
Address: 1-11-22 Omachi, Kamakura City, Kanagawa Pref. Tel: 0467-22-3347

This is one of the oldest shrines in Kamakura, serving as a tutelary shrine to prevent sickness, and was originally called Gion Ten-no-sha. It said that this shrine was built by **Shiragi Saburo Yoshimitsu**, younger brother of Minamoto Yoshiie, the great-great-grandfather of Minamoto Yoritomo.

When Shiragi Saburo stayed in Kamakura on his way to help his brother in a difficult battle in northern Japan from 1082 to 1084, he found the people here were suffering from an epidemic. He therefore asked the Gion Yasaka Shrine monks in Kyoto to perform a ritual prayer to save them. Yasaka shrine was reputed for its ability against all evils, and soon, the epidemic subsided, saving the people. Subsequently, Yasaka Shrine permitted a sub-shrine, named Kamakura Gion-sha, to be built here.

This shrine was later otherwise called Satake-tenno after the Satake family, which enshrined the souls of their ancestors from 1392 to 1428. The Satake family, descendants of Yoshimitsu, also built Joko-myoji temple.

After the Meiji Imperial Restoration in 1868, the Japanese government ordered the segregation of Shinto from Buddhism. Since the word Gion is from Buddhist origin, Gion-sha in Kyoto was forced to change its name and it became Yasaka Shrine. Gion-sha in Kamakura accordingly had to change to "Yakumo Shrine", but popular custom calling it "Gion-san" is still alive in Kamakura. The hiking trail behind the shrine is called "Gion-yama (Mt. Gion) hiking course".

Shinto History

In the Kojiki, the oldest surviving book dealing with Japanese ancient history, there is a myth as told to **Ono-Yasumaro** by **Hieda-no-Are**, in 712, under the order of the Imperial Court, which says that at the very beginning of time there were two gods, Izanagi and Izanami.

"Hereupon all the Heavenly deities commanded the two deities His Augustness the Male-Who-Invites and Her Augustness the Female-Who-Invites, ordering them to make, consolidate, and give birth to this drifting land. Granting to them a heavenly jeweled spear, they thus deigned to charge them. So the two deities, standing upon the Floating Bridge of Heaven pushed down the jeweled spear and stirred with it, whereupon, when they had stirred the brine till it curdled, and drew the spear up, the brine that dripped down from the end of the spear was piled up and became an island. This is the Island of Onogoro."

"Having descended from Heaven on to this island, they saw to the erection of a heavenly august pillar, they saw to the erection of a hall of eight fathoms.

Then Izanagi, the Male-Who-Invites, said to Izanami, the Female-Who-Invites, 'We should create children' and he said, 'Let us go around the heavenly august pillar, and when we meet on the other side let us be united.

Do you go around from the left, and I will go from the right.'

When they met, Her Augustness, the Female-Who-Invites, spake first, exclaiming, 'Ah, what a fair and lovable youth!'

Then His Augustness said, 'Ah what a fair and lovable maiden!'

But afterward he said, 'It was not well that the woman should speak first!'

The child which was born to them was Hiruko (the leech-child), which when three years old was still unable to stand upright. So they placed the leech-child in a boat of reeds and let it float away.

Next they gave birth to the island of Aha. This likewise is not reckoned among their children." [from "Kojiki"]

The next descendants of these gods finally became the legendary emperors of Japan, from **Emperor Jinmu** to **Emperor Suiko**. Based on this myth, the Japanese concept of their empire was thus directly connected to the divine world, and since the 8th century, Japanese worshipped their gods and emperors as the core structure of the nation, or "Kokutai", until the end of World War II. The religion/discipline based on this concept is Shinto.

Shinto has no comprehensive canon or scripture. No written Shinto documents survive from before the seventh century. Japanese worship both in Shinto shrines and Buddhist temples, and don't feel any contradiction from this combination of religions.

Japanese successfully unified the two different faiths from the introduction of Buddhism in the 6th century. A few initial conflicts followed, but the two different religions were soon able to co-exist harmoniously and even complement each other. Many Buddhists even viewed Shinto gods as manifestations of Buddhist deities.

However, this unification was annulled in 1868 by the political transition from feudalism to modernism, the Meiji Restoration. In the Meiji Period, Japan rapidly absorbed Western civilization and industrial technology, and the political leaders embarked on the policy of increasing the nation's economic and military power. This enhanced the rise of nationalism-militarism, and the ideology of Shinto, Japan's state religion, became the backbone of the "divine, chosen-by-god and god-incarnate emperor's nation". Japan's myths of its genesis were used to foster imperialism, and efforts were made to separate and emancipate Shinto from not only Buddhism but also any other culture or religion in the rest of the world. To pay for this ultra-nationalism dominated by militarists, Japan had to sacrifice millions of lives and experience the horrors of World War II.

After the war, Shinto lost its status as the state religion. GHQ (General Head Quarters), the US occupation authorities, issued the Shinto Directive on December 15, 1945, and according to the reformation plan of the Japanese government, the separation of religion and state was declared.

Shinto shrines

The shrine itself, is normally composed of the front oratory part and the rear sanctum part. It is forbidden to go beyond the oratory hall, where all ceremonial prayers are held.

In the sanctum, where it is believed God resides, three symbolic objects are enshrined. They are "Sanshu-no-Jingi", the three sacred treasures. To understand basically what they are, going back to the Genesis of the Japanese Islands would be helpful. **Amaterasu Omi Kami** gave to **Ninigi-no-Mikoto**, three objects; Yata-no-Kagami (a mirror), Ameno-Murakumo-no-Tsurugi (a sword,) and Yasakani-no-Magatama (a jewelled necklace). Ninigi-no-Mikoto was sent to Ashihara-no-Nakatsukuni (Japan), and since then, the mirror has been enshrined in Ise Jingu Shrine, and the sword in Atsuta Jingu Shrine in Nagoya. Only the jewelry has been kept in the Imperial Palace, along with a copy of the mirror made in the time of the 10th Emperor of Japan, **Sujin (BC148-BC30)** and a sword, a replica of the original one preserved at Ise Jingu Shrine. These three sacred treasures, "Sanshu-no-Jingi", have been passed on by successive Emperors of Japan, as proof of the Imperial Throne.

(2) North Area

<Kita Kamakura>

MODEL COURSE (A)	MODEL COURSE (B)
JR Kita-Kamakura Sta. ↓1min. Engakuji ↓10min. Kosho-ji ↓10min. Tokei-ji ↓5min. Jochi-ji ↓10min. Choju-ji ↓ Kencho-ji ↓3min. En-no-ji (all by walking)	JR Kita-Kamakura Sta. ↓1min. Engakuji ↓3min. Yagumo Jinja ↓3min. Hachiman Jinja ↓10min. Jofuku-ji ↓10min. Joraku-ji ↓20min. Kosho-ji ↓10min. Tokei-ji ↓5min. Jochi-ji ↓10min. Choju-ji ↓ Kencho-ji ↓3min. En-no-ji (all by walking)

North

Engaku-ji 円覚寺

Official name: Zuiroku-zan Engaku Kosho Zen-ji
Sect: Rinzai-Shu Engaku-ji sect
Built in 1282
Opened by Mugaku Sogen Bukko Kokushi
Founded by Hojo Tokimune
Principal icon (Hon-zon): Hokan Shaka Nyorai
Open 8:00-17:00 (till 16:00 from November to March)
Entrance fee: ¥200
1 min. from JR Kita-Kamakura Sta.
Address: 409 Yamanouchi, Kamakura City, Kanagawa Pref. Tel: 0467-22-0478

White Heron Pond

The temple's real entrance is situated just in front of JR Kita-Kamakura station. When you enter, on both sides is the legendary Byakuro-chi pond (White Heron Pond), the place where Mugaku from China (then Song Dynasty) arrived having been guided here by a white heron, which was the incarnate spirit of Tsurugaoka-Hachiman-gu Shrine of Kamakura.

Engaku-ji was founded by Hojo Tokimune, the 6th Shogun of the Kamakura Government. Engaku-ji is the head-quarters of Rinzai-shu, Engakuji-sect of Zen denomination and is ranked 2nd in the 5 Great Temples in Kamakura.

Tokimune, who wanted to mourn his soldiers killed in the 1274 and 1281 wars against **Khubilai-khan**'s Mongolian invasion in Kyushu (Southern Japan), invited the Zen priest **Mugaku Sogen** from China (then Song Dynasty) to inaugurate the temple's construction. The name "Engaku" derives from the fact that the canon "Engaku-Kyo" was found in a stone arch at the inauguration of the temple's construction in 1282.

At the beginning, Engaku-ji was a relatively small temple with only one main altar house for asceticism and a monk's residence. However, since it was designated as the government's official temple for worship, it expanded its property through donations of land and buildings. Although it was damaged by a number of fires and earthquakes, the Hojo family never failed to restore the temple each time.

In 1333, the Hojo family collapsed under the attack of **Nitta Yoshisada**. Nev-

San-mon

ertheless, the 15th chief priest **Muso Kokushi** exploited his political ingenuity to succeed in adding seven more halls and 42 subordinate temples (tacchu).

Again in 1374, fire razed the main hall, but four years later, Shogun Ashikaga Ujimitsu of the Muromachi Government helped the temple reconstruct the main altar building.

Those who contributed to building the temple up to the present condition were mainly the Muromachi and Edo Shogunates, who both guaranteed the temple's authority and finances. The temple's property now consists of 60,000 square meters. Engaku-ji's architectural style is typically that of Chinese Zen temples', with almost all the buildings being built in a straight line.

Visitors pass through the principal gate (So-mon) and the temple's gate (San-mon), which was rebuilt in 1783. On the cross beam of this San-mon, hangs the framed plate of the temple's name "Engaku Kosho Zen-ji".

The San-mon signifies the gate of a mountain, as Zen temples are usually built in the mountains.

In the main altar building or "Honden", the principal icon of the temple, a wooden figure of Hokan Shaka Nyorai, is seated on a red lotus flower in the Zen style of "Kekka-fuza" (sitting cross-legged). Contrary to the traditional manner of Nyorai sculptures' simple features, this statue is gaudily dressed and crowned.

Hojo Hyaku-Kan-non

Hojo

The head was made in the Kamakura era, and the body was made in the Edo era. Looking up at the ceiling, one can see the painting "Hakuryu-zu" (White Dragon).

On the left hand side of the altar building, there are two buildings for Zen practice. The first one is called "Senbutsujo", and the second one is called "Kojirin". Ordinary people who want to practice Zen meditation are called Koji, and the Kojirin, in which only Zen practicians are allowed to enter, was built in 1877 by the Master Kosen Zenji.

A special summer Zen lecture course has been held here during the 2nd half of every July since before World War II, in which numerous masters, academics and artists give conferences.

Hojo garden

Butsunichi-an

Going up the left side slope beside the altar building, we find the "Hojo", which was the residence of the temple's chief priest. The front yard of the Hojo is famous for its 33 Kan-non stone statues, "Hyaku-Kan-non ". Some are stone sculptures and some are relief carvings that may amuse visitors by their different expressions and various gestures.

Also in the garden, there is a huge, old juniper tree, which is said to be from the one of seeds that the founder **Mugaku Sogen** brought from China.

Going past the Muso designed pond, "Myoko", on your left we have Butsunichi-an, one of the subordinate temples, which was built as the mausoleum of **Hojo Tokimune**, the 6th Shogun of the Kamakura reign.

In the main building, the wooden statues of Tokimune, his son **Sadatoki** and his grandson **Takatoki** are displayed. It is said that they used to be enshrined in separate mausoleums, but later in Edo era, were brought together here. The wooden statue of Tokimune was possibly made circa 1700 by the priest **Gikai Shosen**.

Butsunichi-an's principal icon, Jizo Bosatsu, is of wooden parquetry made in the Ashikaga era (14th century), as are the statues of Tokimune, Sadatoki and Takatoki that were made later in the Edo era (17th century). In the garden, there are three hermitages called Ensoku-den, Fuko-an and Hoko-den.

Since January 4, 1934, a tea ceremony has been held every month at Ensoku-ken in memory of the virtue of **Hojo Tokimune**, who saved the country from the foreign invasion seven centuries before. Visitors can enjoy tea in the garden and admire the two magnolia trees which Chinese author **Lu Hsun**, (then a student of medicine in Japan) donated in 1931. Butsunichi-an is usually open from 8:00 to 17:00 (from November to March till 16:00), and the entrance fee is ¥100.

Deep behind this Butsunichi-an, we find the oldest and most beautiful Chinese style architecture in Engaku-ji, officially called Man-nen-zan-Shozoku-in.

Shozoku-in over Myoko-chi

Originally, it was built by **Hojo Sadatoki** in

Bell Tower

Bell tower Tea house

1285 to house a tomb for the Busshari (Buddha's ashes) that **Minamoto Sanetomo** received from China (then Song dynasty).

Later, it was given its present name when the former Shozoku-in moved to Engaku-ji from Kencho-ji temple. "Busshari" is kept in the national treasur "Shariden", the oldest work of Tang style architecture in Japan. Although it is not open to the public, one can often hear loud voices of prayer at the entrance door.

After ascending almost 200 steps on the other side of the main altar, we reach the "O-gane" (big bell), one of the three great bells in Kamakura. It is hung in the bell tower at the top of the hill to the south-east of the garden, and is supported by huge old wooden pillars and beams.

We can also enjoy tea and sweets here, and visit a shrine called "Bentendo", which enshrines the Goddess "Benten", a marine God and the protector of "Enoshima" island to the west of Kamakura (near the Koshigoe beach). This hilltop affords a beautiful view of Mt.Fuji beyond the foothills.

Tacchu

In Zen Buddhist tradition, when a greatly respected Zen master passes away, his followers used to build a hut beside his tomb in memory of the master's life-time teachings. That is called Tacchu or Tatto, a branch or subordinate temple.

Some masters used to build their Tacchu by themselves even when they were still alive. Because priests serve Hotoke (Buddha), they must stay in the temple forever, even after their death.

Throughout the long history of Engaku-ji, there have been many great masters, and consequently a great number of Tacchu have been built within or near the temple. They are built in the depths of the woods or mountains and contain many important statues and artistic objects of national importance. Although some of them are not open to the public, the following temples are "Tacchu" of Engaku-ji.

Keisho-an (Engaku-ji Tacchu) 桂昌庵

Official name: Keisho-an
Sect: Rinzai-shu Engaku-ji sect
Opened for Shosen Dokin

Principal icon: Yagara Jizo
Open 8:00-17:00 (till 16:00 from November to March)
1 min. from JR Kita-Kamakura Sta.
Address: 490 Yamanouchi, Kamakura City, Kanagawa Pref.

The temple's treasures are the statues of ten infernal Gods of judgement; Shinko, Shogo, Sotei, Gokan, Enma, Henjo, Taizan, Byodo, Toshi and Godo-Tenrin. It is said that a dead person has to be judged by those ten Gods to have his final destination decided. The statues were made around 1717, in the Edo era. Keisho-an's Japanese archery (Kyudo) dojo is open to the public.

Japanese archery

Yabusame

Yabusame is a competition of archery skills on horseback, traditionally done by samurai. Nowadays, this exciting sport is performed by skilled riders in ancient hunting costumes, who shoot arrows at fixed targets about 70m apart as they gallop down the 260m track in quick succession.

This ritual event once disappeared, but in 1922 was revived by the efforts of an expert archer, **Honda Seifuku**. This very popular event is held on the 3rd Sunday of April, during the Kamakura Spring Festival, and in mid September, during the shrine's annual festival.

The warriors of Kamakura excelled at shooting on horseback. Even in peacetime, samurai had to improve their martial skills, including Yabusame, and it was a great honor to participate in this competition, started by Yoritomo in 1187.

Fuyo-an (Engaku-ji Tacchu) 富陽庵

Official name: Fuyo-an
Sect: Rinzai-Shu Engaku-ji sect
Built by Uesugi Asamune for Togaku Bun-iku in circa 1400
Principal icon: Monju Bosatsu
Not open to the public
3 min. from JR Kita-Kamakura Sta.
Address: On Engakuji grounds

This is the tomb/temple of the 61st chief priest,

Togaku Bun-iku, who passed away in 1416. He first lived in Jufuku-ji before coming to Engaku–ji. In the temple, are statues of Togaku Bun-iku and **Tokei Tokugo**, the 4th chief priest of Engakuji. Tokei Tokugo was a Zen monk who studied in Song China and came back to Japan with **Mugaku Sogen**, the Chinese priest who inaugurated Engaku-ji.

Densho-an (Engaku-ji Tacchu)　伝宗庵

Official name: Denshu-an
Sect: Rinzai-Shu Engaku-ji sect
Built in 1317 for Nanzan Shiun
Principal icon: Jizo Bosatsu
Not open to the public
2 min. from JR Kita-kamakura Sta.
Address: In Engaku-ji property

Kita-Kamakura Kindergarten

The founder, **Nanzan Shiun**, was the 11th chief priest of Engaku-ji. The wooden statue of Jizo Bosatsu (a national cultural asset) is characterised by its decorative flower design of camelia and ume blossoms, made of molded earth. The body was constructed in parquetry technique, and has jewels for eyes. The statue is now kept in the Kamakura National Treasure Museum. The temple's site is used by Kita-Kamakura Kindergarten.

Haku-un-an (Engaku-ji Tacchu)　白雲庵

Official name: Haku-un-an
Sect: Rinzai-Shu Engaku-ji sect
Opened for Tomin Enichi
Built around 1312-1316 by Hojo Sadatoki
Principal icon: Hokan Shaka Nyorai
Not open to the public
4 min. from JR Kita-kamakura Sta.
Address: 462 Yamanouchi, Kamakura City, Kanagawa Pref. Tel: 0467-22-5009

The 10th chief priest of Engaku-ji, **Tomin Enichi**, came to Kamakura from

China (Song dynasty) in 1309 by invitation of **Hojo Sadatoki**. He was a Soto sect monk (not Rinzai), but the temple shifted to Rinzai sect later in the Muromachi era.

The principal icon is of wooden parquetry, jewel-eyed and japanned, as is the statue of Enichi. The temple is situated next to Uncho-an.

Sculpture by Isamu Noguchi

Uncho-an (Engaku-ji Tacchu) 雲頂庵

Official name: Daiki-san Uncho-an
Sect: Rinzai-Shu Engaku-ji sect
Opened for Kusan En-in
Built in 1282
Re-founded by Tadakage Nagao
Principal icon: Hokan Shaka Nyorai
Not open to the public
5 min. from JR Kita-Kamakura Sta.
Address: 479 Yamanouchi Kamakura City, Kanagawa Pref. Tel: 0467-22-3904

Originally the Uncho-an was the subordinate temple of Chosho-ji which was one of the ten greatest temples in the Kanto area. The passage to Uncho-an can be found some blocks back from the Engaku-ji main gate toward Ofuna Station.

The master **Kusan En-in** was the founder of Chosho-ji Temple. As Chosho-ji was closed toward 1438, Uncho-an also was abolished. However, years later, **Nagao Tadakage** rebuilt the temple.

The main wooden icon, Hokan Shaka Nyorai, is said to have had its head made in the Edo era and the body in Muromachi era. The statue of the founder Kusan En-in is the other main temple treasure.

Shorei-in (Engaku-ji Tacchu) 松嶺院

Official name: Entsu-zan Shorei-in
Sect: Rinzai-shu Engaku-ji sect
Opened for Ko-en Myokan
Principal icon: Shakamuni-butsu
Open 8:00-17:00 in April, May, June, July, September,

October and November (In November open till 16:00)
Entrance fee: ¥100
2 min. from JR Kita-Kamakura Sta.
Address: 453 Yamanouchi, Kamakura City, Kanagawa Pref.

Past the main gate, the second temple on the left hand side is the Shorei-in, built by Engaku-ji's 150th chief priest, **Ko-en Myokan**, who passed away in 1535. It was formerly called Fukanken, but the name was changed to the present one when a nun, Shorei-in, donated the property to the temple.

It is said that on this temple's site, there used to be another temple called Seisho-an, which was the tacchu of the 44th chief priest Daisetsu Sono.

In the cemetery of the temple, the famous movie actress **Tanaka Kinuyo**, writer **Kaiko Ken** and the family of the **lawyer Sakamoto** who were killed by the fanatic religious sect Aum Shinri-kyo, are at rest.

Ryoin-an (Engaku-ji Tacchu) 龍隠庵

Official name: Ryoin-an
Sect: Rinzai-shu Engaku-ji sect
Built in 1419 by Hoin Shogiku
Opened for Taiga Shoin
Principal icon: Sei Kanzeon Bosatsu
4 min. from JR Kita-Kamakura Sta.
Address: 450 Yamanouchi, Kamakura City, Kanagawa Pref. Tel: 0467-25-1447

Ryoin-an garden

A tiny stone stairway between the Senbutsu-jo and the Kojirin, leads up to the Ryoin-an, built in 1419 by **Hoin Shogiku**. This is one of Engakuji's subordinate temples, where **Taiga Shoin**, the 102nd head priest of Engaku-ji, is buried. The house doors are open, and you can see its tiny one foot high principal icon, "Sei Kanzeon Bosatsu", through the window.

In the front garden, visitors can enjoy free tea service sitting on red carpeted benches, with a view of the Honden's green copper roof and Kojirin's thatched roof against the green hillside. In February, the red and white blossoms of the Ume (Japanese apricot) trees are welcome signs of early spring.

Shozoku-in (Engaku-ji Tacchu)　正続院

Official name: Man-nen-zan Shozoku-in
Sect: Rinzai-shu Engaku-ji sect
Opened for Mugaku Sogen in 1285
Principal icon: Jizo Bosatsu
Not open to the public
5 min. from JR Kita-Kamakura Sta.
Address: In Engaku-ji property

Originally, this temple was built by **Hojo Sadatoki** in 1285 with the name of Shosho-ji, as a place to keep Buddha's ashes (Busshari). It is said that the Buddha's ashes were brought from China in the Song Dynasty and offered to **Minamoto Sanetomo**. Later, the temple was converted to a memorial hall for Mugaku Sogen, the founder of Engaku-ji, and the name was then changed to the present one.

The temple is not only home to the Buddha's ashes in Shariden Hall, but also has a Zen meditation practice hall, Shoho Gendo, for younger monks.

Sai-in-an (Engaku-ji Tacchu)　済蔭庵

Official name: Sai-in-an
Sect: Rinzai-Shu Engaku-ji sect
Opened for Donbo Shu-o
Principal icon: Fudo Myo-o
Not open to the public except for Zen meditation circle members.
3 min. from JR Kita-Kamakura Sta.
Address: In Engaku-ji property

Donbo Shu-o was the direct disciple of **Muso Soseki** and the 56th Engaku-ji chief priest. Today, the temple is a Zen meditation Dojo named "Kojirin", open to the public for regular weekend practice. Koji signifies a lay Zen practician.

Jutoku-an (Engaku-ji Tacchu) 寿徳庵

Official name: Nan-zan Jutoku-an
Sect: Rinzai-Shu Engaku-ji sect
Opened for Gettan Chu-en
Rebuilt by Miura Dosun
Principal icon: Sei Kanzeon Bosatsu
Not open to the public
4 min. from JR Kita-Kamakura Sta.
Address: 444 Yamanouchi, Kamakura City, Kanagawa Pref. Tel: 0467-24-0808

This is the tacchu temple of the 66th chief priest, **Gettan Chu-en**, who became the chief priest of Engaku-ji after serving in Zuisen-ji. The temple contains a statue of Chu-en that was made in 1810.

In the temple's cemetery, we can see the tombs of the Miura family, which collapsed when **Miura Dosun** was killed by **Hojo So-un** (Shogun of the Muromachi Reign) in 1516.

Shoden-an (Engaku-ji Tacchu) 正伝庵

Official name: Shoden-an
Sect: Rinzai-Shu Engaku-ji sect
Built by Myogan Sho-in Daitatsu Zenji in 1348
Principal icon: Hokan Shaka
Not open to the public
5 min. from JR Kita-Kamakura Sta.
Address: In Engaku-ji property

Shoden-an was built as the tomb for **Myogan Sho-in**, the 24th chief priest of Engaku-ji temple. According to the signature found in the sculpture's body, we know precisely that the statue of Myogan Sho-in was made in 1365 when he was 81 years old.

Another treasure of the temple, Hokan Shaka, was made in the Ashikaga Reign (14th and 15th centuries). Hokan means "crowned" and Shaka is the Japanese name of **Gautama Siddhartha (Buddha's real name)**.

Zokuto-an (Engaku-ji Tacchu)　続燈庵

Official name: Manpu-zan Zokuto-an
Sect: Rinzai-Shu Engaku-ji sect
Built in 1362 for Daiki Hokin Butsuman Zenji
Principal icon: Kan-non Bosatsu
Not open to the public
6 min. from JR Kita-Kamakura Sta.
Address: 431 Yamanouchi, Kamakura City, Kanagawa Pref. Tel: 0467-22-9355

Daiki Hokin was the 30th chief priest of Engaku-ji, after serving as the chief priest of Jomyo-ji. The main icon, Kanzeon Bosatsu, was originally enshrined in Tokei-ji.

Obai-in (Engaku-ji Tacchu)　黄梅院

Official name: Den-ne-san Obai-in
Sect: Rinzai-Shu Engaku-ji sect
Built in 1354 for Muso Soseki
Founded by Aeba Ujinao
Principal icon: Senju Kan-non Bosatsu
Open 8:00-17:00 (till 16:00 from November to March)
6 min. from JR Kita-Kamakura Sta.
Address: 428 Yamanouchi, Kamakura City, Kanagawa Pref. Tel: 0467-22-1032

The master **Muso Soseki** contributed greatly to Zen literature, and was aided and protected by **Ashikaga Takauji**, the Shogun of the Muromachi reign. After the 2nd Shogun, **Ashikaga Yoshiakira**'s, ashes were entrusted here, Obai-in became the Ashikaga's family temple.

It is also one of Engaku-ji's subordinate temples. The main icon's name, "Senju", signifies a thousand hands, because the statue has 18 arms. Obai means yellow blossom of the Japanese apricot "Ume".

Nyoi-an (Engaku-ji Tacchu)　如意庵

Official name: Nyoi-an

Sect: Rinzai-Shu Engaku-ji sect
Opened for Muge Myoken Busshin Zenji
Built in 1370 by Uesugi Daisuke Noriaki
Principal icon: Hokan Shaka Nyorai
Not open to the public
5 min. from JR Kita-Kamakura Sta.
Address: 425 Yamanouchi, Kamakura City, Kanagawa Pref. Tel: 0467-22-7211

Muge Myoken was the 36th chief priest of Engaku-ji, and the temple was opened the year after he passed away.

The dragon painting on the ceiling has a ball that gives off various colors when seen from different angles.

Kigen-in (Engaku-ji Tacchu) 帰源院

Official name: Kigen-in
Sect: Rinzai-Shu Engaku-ji sect
Opened for Ketsuo Ze-ei in circa 1378
Principal icon: Ketsuo Ze-ei
Not open to the public
4 min. from JR Kita-Kamakura Sta.
Address: 416 Yamanouchi, Kamakura City, Kanagawa Pref.

The 38th chief priest, **Ketsuo Ze-ei**, is buried in this temple. He also served in Taikei-ji in Ofuna and in Jochi-ji as chief priest.

The famous writer **Natsume Soseki** (author of "I am a Cat") took part in Zen meditation here in 1894, and wrote the novel "Mon" (The gate) after this experience. The temple has a beautiful thatched roof gate and a pleasant garden.

Garyo-an (Engaku-ji Tacchu) 臥龍庵

Official name: Garyo-an
Sect: Rinzai-shu Engaku-ji sect
Opened for Daisen Dotsu
Built in 1338 or 1339

Principal icon: Daisen Dotsu
Not open to the public
1 min. from JR Kita-Kkamakura Sta.
Address: 410 Yamanouchi, Kamakura City, Kanagawa
Pref. Tel: 0467-22-9218

This is the memorial temple for **Daisen Dotsu**, the 16th chief priest of Engaku-ji. The temple, situated on the right hand side just outside of the main gate, facing the train track, contains the wooden statue of Daisen Dotsu, made in the 14th century.

Zen Buddhism and Kamakura

Zen Buddhism was introduced from Tibet to China by the Master, Dharma, in the middle of the 6th century. Over the following centuries, Zen Buddhism developed into various sects in China, and by the Song dynasty, it had reached its prime.

The beginning of Zen Buddhism in Japan came when the **Master Eisai**, introduced Rinzai Zen toward the 2nd half of the 12th century (Kamakura era) from China (then Song Dynasty). Some decades later, another mainstream of Zen, Soto sect, was brougt to Japan from China in 1227 by the **Master Dogen**.

The principle of Zen Buddhism is that the spirit of Buddha can only be mastered by Zazen (Zen meditation), in another words, direct inspiration and communication with the truth without depending on scholarly studies or being taught by others.

The Kamakura Shogunate was the first warrior (Samurai or Bushi) reign in Japan, and was spiritually different from the central Kyoto imperial-aristocratic government which was authoritative and conservative, yet at the same time and culturaly-based and weak-hearted. The warrior tradition of the Minamoto and Hojo families' Samurai found in Zen Buddhism the most important moral prop and stay of its basis for political and social leadership.

Hojo Tokimune was such an ardent Zen believer that he founded Engaku-ji temple as the principal temple of the Kamakura government.

Engaku-ji's first head priest, Mugaku Sogen, was Tokimune's spiritual master, who morally sustained him at the time of the Mongolian invasions of Kyushu.

Yagumo Jinja (Yamanouchi)　八雲神社

Official name: Yagumo Jinja
Enshrined Gods: Suasano-no-Mikoto
Founded in 1224

Distinctive property: Good luck, quick recovery from illness, protection of agriculture and industry, good connections
Annual festival: July 15
Sub shrine: Inari-sha
5 min. from JR Kita-Kamakura Sta.
Address: 585 Yamanouchi, Kamakuta City, Kanagawa Pref.

Magical Stone of Abe Haruaki

This is the Chinju of the Yamanouchi community. In the Kamakura era, when an epidemic struck the capital, ritual prayers took place everywhere to fight the disease. The people tried to evoke the spirit of Gion Yasaka shrine in Kyoto and prayed for the safety and peace of the community. This formed the basis of the shrine. Later in the Muromachi era, the governor of eastern Japan, **Uesugi Norifusa**, also worshipped in this spirit.

The stone monument "Koshinto", erected in 1665, is the biggest and oldest in Kamakura. The stone of Haruaki is another curiosity. This stone was found in a road construction site and assumed to be the stone enshrined by **Abe Haruaki**, a charismatic fortune teller of the Heian period. The stone is said to have power against disaster and must be kept clean and treated with respect.

Hachiman Jinja　八幡神社

Official name: Hachiman Jinja
Enshrined Gods: Emperor Ojin
Founded in 1735
Virtue: Family safety
Annual festival: July 22
5 min. from JR Kita-Kamakura Sta.
Address: 2044 Dai, Kamakura City, Kanagawa Pref.

On the left hand side of Engaku-ji, after passing through a tunnel and following a very narrow path between the houses, you should be able to find this shrine. According to the shrine's historical records, the lord of this area, Bessho, asked Iwashimizu Hachiman-gu for permission to build a branch shrine here.

The local people call this shrine "Sho-Hachiman-sama" (Little Hachiman God), and it is the guardian shrine (Chinju) of Dai commercial area.

In old times, on the 5th and 10th of every month, a Benihana flower market was held in the Dai marketplace, and in the Edo era, a horse market was also held.

Jofuku-ji　成福寺

Official name: Kikko-zan Hotoku-in Jofuku-ji
Sect: Jodo-shin-Shu
Inaugurated and built by Jobutsu in 1232
Principal icon: Amida Nyorai
15 min. from JR Kita-Kamakura Sta.
Address: 2-13-33 Kobukuroya, Kamakura City, Kanagawa Pref. Tel: 0467-46-3020

On the other side of the Yokosuka Line railway at Kobukuroya crossing, facing the railway track stands Jofuku-ji, which is the only Jodo-shin-shu temple in Kamakura. Jodo-shin-shu was established by **Master Shinran**, who was a disciple of **Master Honen**, the founder of Jodo-shu. "Shin" signifies the most "genuine" school of Jodo-shu. In the main hall, together with the principal icon, Amida Nyorai, the painted icons of the founder Shinran and his successor, **Ren-nyo**, are displayed. One of the temple treasures is the wooden statue of **Prince Shotoku**, which was made in the late Kamakura era. Jodo-shu reveres Prince Shotoku, who was a strong reformer in 6th to 7th century Japan and a devout Buddhist. Treasures also include hanging scrolls of calligraphy by Shinran and Ren-nyo.

The founder of the temple, Jobutsu's, real name was **Hojo Yasutsugu**. He was the son of **Hojo Yasutoki**, the 3rd Regent of the Kamakura Shogunate. He first became a monk of the Tendai-shu and later followed Shinran. The statue of Prince Shotoku is said to have been donated by Shinran to Jobutsu when he converted to Jodo-shin-shu.

Jofuku-ji became masterless after the Kamakura shogunate collapsed, and stayed masterless until the Muromachi era 70 years later.

Joraku-ji 常楽寺

Main gate

Monju-do Hall

Official name: Zokusen-zan Joraku-ji
Sect: Rinzai-Shu Kencho-ji sect
Inaugurated by Taiko Gyoyu in 1237
Built by Hojo Yasutoki
Principal icon: Amida Sanzon
Open: 9:00-16:30
20 min. from JR Ofuna Sta. east exit or Kita-Kamakura Sta.
Address: 5-8-29 Ofuna, Kamakura City, Kanagawa Pref. Tel: 0467-46-5735

The first part of the temple's name, Zokusen-zan, can be otherwise read as "Awafune" in Japanese, which means a millet barge. In old times, a major part of the Ofuna area was covered by water, and large boats transporting grains and other commodities could easily dock there. Awafune is said to be the origin of the name Ofuna.

Hojo Yasutoki built a hall here, inaugurated by **Taiko Gyoyu**, to mourn his mother-in-law's passing.

The temple has a close relationship with the founder of Kencho-ji, **Rankei Doryu**, who had started to teach Zen Buddhism in this temple in 1248, five years before Kencho-ji was built.

The remaining buildings are the main hall, the main gate and the Monju-do Hall. In the main hall, the principal icon, Amida Nyorai, the two asistant Bosatsu, Kan-non and Seji, and the statue of Rankei Doryu are enshrined.

On the ceiling of the hall, we can admire the painting of "Unryu" (Dragon in the cloud) by **Kano Yukinobu**. The dragon in this painting has no eyes, which are said to have been lost because he moved around too much during the night.

The bell is made of bronze and is ranked one of the three great bells in Kamakura, together with those of Engaku-ji and Kencho-ji.

The pond, Shikiten Munetsu and Zen style garden are also not to be missed.

Behind the main hall, we can see the tomb of the founder, Hojo Yasutoki and the 13th chief priest of Kencho-ji, **Nanbo Jomin**.

Kosho-ji 光照寺

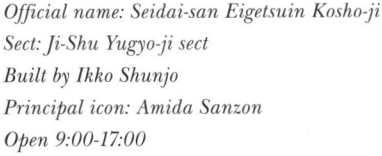

Official name: Seidai-san Eigetsuin Kosho-ji
Sect: Ji-Shu Yugyo-ji sect
Built by Ikko Shunjo
Principal icon: Amida Sanzon
Open 9:00-17:00
5 min. from JR Kita-Kamakura Sta.
Address: 827 Yamanouchi, Kamakura City, Kanagawa Pref. Tel: 0467-46-6355

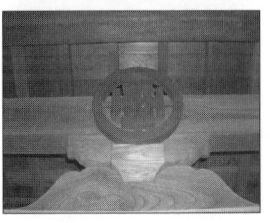

Crest of the cross

The Ji-shu sect was founded by **Ippen**, one of the "Great Vehicle" Buddhism masters. Ippen built Yugyo-ji (Official name: Shojo-ko-ji) and this Kosho-ji is its subordinate temple.

At this temple, people come to pray for the sake of their children. Beside the main gate, stands a Jizo called Kosodate Jizo which is believed to make all the wishes for the sake of the children come true.

Curiously enough, there is a crest of a Christian cross hung above the beam of the temple's gate. Also, two candle stands of early Christians in Japan are preserved in the main altar house, which was built in 1859. By this fact, we can assume that in the Edo era, there were a certain number of Christians in Kamakura, although it was strictly forbidden. It is not yet clear how and why the Ji-shu Buddhists would protect Christians.

Tokei-ji 東慶寺

Official name: Shokozan Tokei Soji Zen-ji
Sect: Rinzai-Shu Engaku-ji sect
Inaugurated in 1285 by Kakuzan Shido-ni
Built by Hojo Sadatoki
Principal icon: Shaka Nyorai
Open 8:30-17:00 (summer) 8:30-16:00 (winter)
Treasure museum 10:00-15:00 (closed on Monday, open holidays)
Entrance fee: ¥100
Treasure museum: ¥300

3min. from JR Kita-Kamakura Sta.
Address: 1367 Yamanouchi, Kamakura City, Kanagawa Pref. Tel: 0467-22-1653

This temple, which was opened as a nunnery by **Kakuzan-ni** ("ni" means a nun), the wife of **Hojo Tokimune**, became famous as a place of refuge for women in trouble. In ancient times, a wife could not divorce her abusive husband without the permission of the husband himself. Women in such trouble used to run into this temple, and if they stayed for three years, were entitled to a divorce by the law of the temple. This law was abolished in 1871, as the Shogunate ended, and in 1903, the temple was converted from a nunnery to a Rinzai sect Zen temple.

It is also famous for its flower garden and its many precious decorative articles from different epochs of history, including the valuable "Suigetsu Kannon" statue, in the treasure museum. (Reservation is necessary.)

Jochi-ji　浄智寺

Official name: Kinpo-zan Jochi-ji
Sect: Rinzai-Shu Engaku-ji sect
Inaugurated in 1281 by Nanshu Kokai-Honen, Daikyu Shonen and Gottan Funei
Built by Hojo Morotoki
Principal icon: Sanzebutsu Nyorai
Open 9:00-16:30
Entrance fee: ¥150
8 min. from JR Kita-Kamakura Sta.
Address: 1402 Yamanouchi, Kamakura City, Kanagawa Pref. Tel: 0467-22-3943

This temple was founded by the widow and son of Hojo Munemasa to mourn the deceased 3rd son of Hojo Tokiyori. The temple is ranked 4th of the Five Great Temples in Kamakura.

The initial buildings were burnt down in 1356, and rebuilt in the Muromachi era (1338-1573) with a great number of new buildings.

Again in the 20th century, the Great Earthquake of 1923 destroyed almost the entire temple. Since then, the temple has been reconstructed little by little to regain its original beautiful appearance. The bell tower here is placed on top of the gate, which is rarely seen in temple architecture. This style is called "Shoro-mon".

The temple's enormous property is so rich in vegetation that it is preserved as a national historic site, and taking a walk throughout the grounds in each of the four seasons is highly recommended.

Hotei's frequently stroked belly

The main icon, Sanzebutsu Nyorai, is actually three statues of the Gods Amida, Shaka and Miroku, the symbols of the past, the present and the future, respectively. They are designated as national cultural assets.

Behind the cemetery is a grotto where the Hotei stone statue stands. It is one of the Shichifuku-jin (Seven Lucky Gods), and if we pat his fat round belly, we are assured of good luck.

Kanro-no-i <10 Famous Wells of Kamakura>

This well is found just in front of the main gate of Jochi-ji temple. There is a tiny stone bridge over a pond. Beside the pond, a well covered with bamboo canes can be found. Kanro means sweet water drops and the water sustained daily life for people in the neighborhood in old times.

Meigetsu-in　明月院

Official name: Fukugenzan Meigetu-in
Sect: Rinzai-Shu Kencho-ji sect
Inaugurated by Misshitsu Shugon in 1160
Built by Uesugi Norikata
Principal icon: Sei Kanzeon Bosatsu
Open 9:00-16:00
Entrance fee: ¥300
10min. from JR Kita-Kamakura Sta.
Address: 189 Yamanouchi, Kamakura City, Kana-

65

gawa Pref. Tel: 0467-24-3437

Before **Minamoto Yoritomo** established the Kamakura Shogunate, a samurai family called Yamanouchi was already living in the Kita-Kamakura area, and the area still carries this as a place-name.

Originally a tiny house, Meigetsu-an, was built to mourn **Shuto Toshimochi**, who had been killed in the war against the Taira family. The victor in this war was the Minamoto family, and one hundred years later, the Hojo family took over the power in Kamakura. The governor, **Hojo Tokiyori**, built a temple, "Saimyo-ji", on this place in 1256. He became a monk and lived in Saimyo-ji until his death in 1263.

After Tokiyori's death, his son Tokimune settled this temple officially as a Zen temple and renamed it Zenko-ji.

Therefore, Meigetsu-an temple and Saimyo-ji temple were together on this site for another 100 years.

In 1380, during the Ashikaga reign, when the governor of this province, **Uesugi Norikata**, expanded the temple's territory and made further improvements, the former Meigetsu-an was promoted and renamed Meigetsu-in.

Zenko-ji, built by Tokimune, also existed with Meigetsu-in for four centuries and was even once ranked as the top of the ten greatest temples in Eastern Japan. However, it was finally abolished in the Meiji Restoration of 1867. In the main altar house, called "Hojo", we can find the principal icon, Sei Kanzeon Bosatsu. The inaugurator, Misshitsu Shugon's statue is in the So-yu-do. At the right hand side of the So-yu-do, one of the Ten Wells in Kamakura, called "Tsurube-No-I", is still in use.

Above all, this temple has become quite famous over the past few decades for its beautiful hydrangea flowers, which bloom in the June-July rainy season.

Choju-ji (Kencho-ji Tacchu)　長寿寺

Official name: Hoki-zan Choju-ji

Sect: Rinzai-Shu Kencho-ji sect
Built between 1329-1331 for Ashikaga Takauji
Inaugurated by Kosen Ingen
Founded by Ashikaga Motouji
Principal icon: Kan-non Bosatsu
Open: 10:00 to 15:00ÐFriday, Saturday, Sunday from March during JuneÐ
Entrance fee: ¥300
10 min. from JR Kita-Kamakura Sta.
Address: 1503 Yamanouchi, Kamakura City, Kanagawa Pref. Tel: 0467-22-2147

The temple was constructed on the land where **Ashikaga Takauji**, the 1st Shogun of the Muromachi Reign, had his residence. "Choju" was Takauji's name as a priest after he retired in his old age.

The original temple was quite large and had seven buildings, but according to historical records, it was lost in a fire in December 1448. The temple was founded by Ashikaga Motouji, the first governor in Kamakura, to pray for the repose of his father, Takauji.

The founding priest, **Kosen Ingen (1295-1374)**, came to Kamakura from Kagoshima Prefecture, in the southern part of Kyushu, when he was only eight years old, and entered Engaku-ji to became a priest. He took the tonsure at age 13 and visited China at 24 to study Buddhism, staying there for eight years. In 1326, he returned to Kamakura together with a Chinese Zen priest named **Seicho Seisetsu**. Seisetsu was then invited to Kencho-ji to succeed the post of the 22nd chief priest.

After serving at Kencho-ji, Jochi-ji and other temples, Seisetsu was invited to become the 29th chief priest of Engaku-ji in 1359 and later the 38th chief priest of Kencho-ji. His top disciple, Kosen, was nominated to be the inaugurating priest of Choju-ji.

In Kan-non-do Hall, a statue of Sho-Kan-non is enshrined in the rather small structure with a thatched roof. The temple also has a statue of Priest Kosen, and a statue of **Ashikaga Takauji**, both made during the Muromachi Era.

Behind the main hall is a Gorinto for Takauji, in which his hair is said to be preserved as a keepsake.

Now, there is Hondo (main temple) newly built in 2006.

Kamakura and the Flourishing of Buddhism

Buddhism was introduced into Japan from China through Pekche (ancient Korea) in the mid 6th century. Despite the boycotting by the indigenous tribal forces, Buddhism spread over Japan and finally managed to convert the imperial family to Buddhism toward the end of the same century. In the 8th century, Buddhism in Japan became even more prosperous, and many great masters appeared and many temples were constructed as well. From the political point of view, one can say that Buddhism played an important part in unifying the nation.

Zen Buddhism, such as Rinzai and Soto denominations, was originally established at the beginning of the 11th century in China in the flourishing Song Dynasty (10th to 13th century). Zen Buddhism was brought to Japan by the **Master Eisai** as the Rinzai Zen denomination in 1191 from China. Thereafter, Buddhism in Japan began to develop in its own way. Over several hundred years, many great masters appeared and established many different denominations and sects.

In the 2nd half of the 12th century, the **Master Honen** started his denomination "Jodo-shu" and **Nichiren** established his Nichiren-shu a little later in the same century.

Historically speaking, the Kamakura Shogunate was Japan's first reign by a Samurai government, and was also a very properous time for culture and religion, largely under the Chinese influence.

Many Kamakura Zen monks were keen intellectuals who excelled in literature, poetry, essays, diaries, travelologues etc.. Thus, the Kamakura period is considered the Golden Age of Chinese Literature in Japan.

Order of the five Great Temples in Kamakura

1. Kencho-ji
2. Engaku-ji
3. Jufuku-ji
4. Jochi-ji
5. Jomyo-ji

(The Hojo government started the promotion system of temples and priests for political reasons in order to tightly control the growing popularity of Zen temples.)

Kencho-ji　建長寺

Official name: Kofuku-san Kencho Kokoku Zen-ji
Sect: Rinzai-Shu Kencho-ji sect
Inaugurated by Rankei Do-ryu
Built in 1253 by Hojo Tokiyori
Principal icon: Jizo Bosatsu
Open 8:30-16:30

Entrance fee: ¥300
15 min. from JR Kita-Kamakura Sta.
Address: 8 Yamanouchi, Kamakura City, Kanagawa
Pref. Tel: 0467-22-0981

Kencho-ji is the head temple (dai-honzan) and the first ranked of the Five Great Temples in Kamakura. The temple's name "Kencho" derives from the Kencho period in the Japanese calendar, "Nen-go", of the year it was built. The name Kofukusan comes from the name of the sloping road, "Kobukuro-zaka", that passes in front of the temple.

Butsu-den

The inaugurator, **Rankei Do-ryu**, was a Chinese Zen monk from Setuang. Inspired by a Japanese student-monk he met in China, he took a boat to Japan, landing at Hakata (Kyushu), in 1246, and then went to Kyoto before coming to Kamakura. He first stayed in Jufuku-ji, the Rinzai Zen temple built by **Eisai**. Later he met **Hojo Tokiyori**, the 5th Kamakura Shogun, who eventually ordered him to build the first Zen temple in Japan.

Rankei taught Zen very as severely as it was taught in his home country, Song. According to the manuscript written by Rankei, practitioners had to meditate for 9 hours a day and those who made a noise or talked when walking received severe punishment. This tradition is still observed today in the temple's Zen dojo, but the details of the Zen practice in Kencho-ji are not open to the public.

After passing through the main gate, the second two storied Gate, called Sanmon (national cultural asset) solemnly receives visitors. On its first floor, the statues of Shaka Nyorai and five hundred Rakan (Gohyaku Rakan, the 500 Buddha disciples who compiled the cannon after his death) are kept. They are displayed to the public every year around November 3 at the occasion of "Homotsu Kazeire" (treasure cleaning and ventilation) event.

The reason the temple's main icon is Jizo Bosatsu, a rarity in Zen temples, stems from the nature of the site where the temple was constructed.

In old times, the place was an execution site, called "Jigoku-dani" (Hell Valley). Jizo Bosatsu

Jizo Bosatsu

Hatto

is believed to be a God who saves the spirits of those who have fallen into hell. The Jizo Bosatsu found in the main altar house has a height of 2.40m, and counting its platform reaches to 4.80m. It is exceptionally grandiose and gorgeous for a simple, modest Zen temple.

The Jizo Bosatsu holds a cane in his right hand and a treasure ball called Hoju in his left, which is a standard Jizo posture. Jizo accompanies the deceased till the trial before Enma, and defends him or her by making excuses. Its popular name, "Excuse Jizo", is derived from this story.

This Jizo Bosatsu had another smaller Jizo called "Saita Jizo" in its bosom. Once upon a time, a certain Saita Saemon was about to be executed after being falsely accused. However, the executor's sword broke each time they tried to kill him, and no one could understand what was happening. Then Saita Saemon told them.

"I devoutly believe in Jizo. I always go with him. I keep him in my hair. You can never kill me since my Jizo protects me."

They looked into his hair and found a tiny Jizo statue with several wounds. The execution was suspended and Saita was released. He offered his Jizo statue to the Jizo Bosatsu's bosom of Shinpei-ji. When Kencho-ji was built, Shinpei-ji was moved to another place and the Jizo Bosatsu was kept here as the main icon.

Karamon gate

Hojo garden

Just behind the Butsu-den is the "Hatto" built in 1814. One can contemplate the precious "Senju Kan-non" through its window. It is said that Senju Kan-non has a thousand hands and a thousand eyes of mercy to save the people from misery and disaster.

Behind Hatto is Hojo with its beautiful Karamon gate. On the right hand side of the Karamon-gate, one can go through to enter Hojo and have a tranquil moment contemplating the Zen garden, with Shinji-no-Ike pond in the middle, designed in the shape of the letter Kokoro (heart).

During the Kamakura period, all the buildings in this temple were connected to each other by roofed corridors, and the entire temple was composed symmetrically in the Chinese architectural style. However, many of the buildings were destroyed or burnt because of earthquakes and fires during the 14th and 15th centuries. The present temples and other buildings were rebuilt in the Edo era.

If one keeps on going deep into the back mountain, the path becomes a bit steeper and finally reaches the long stone stairways to Hanzobo Shrine up the valley of Shojoken Mountain. It was built in 1890 as a tutelary shrine for Kencho-ji. This mountain is 114m high and has a quite enjoyable 2 hour hiking trail from here to the mountain behind Zuisen-ji temple.

Zen cooking is well known for its vegetarian simplicity and Kencho-ji's long tradition has created a very popular soup called "Kenchin-jiru", which is a light miso soup with burdock, raddish, carrot, taro potato and tofu. There is a restaurant that serves Kenchin-jiru in front of the temple's gate.

Myoko-in (Kencho-ji Tacchu)　妙高院

Official name: Jakusho-zan Myoko-in
Sect: Rinzai-Shu Kencho-ji sect
Built circa 1346 by Kozan Mongo Kakukai Zenji
Principal icon: Hokan Shaka Nyorai
Not open to the public
15 min. from JR Kita-Kamakura Sta.
Address: 9 Yamanouchi, Kamakura City, Kanagawa Pref. Tel: 0467-25-1005

Kozan Mongo was the 28th chief priest of Kencho-ji. He successively filled the chief priest post of numerous importants temples, such as Sangen-ji in Hizen (Kumamoto Pref. in Kyushu), Saizen-ji in Kyoto and Zenpuku-ji in Sagami (Kanagawa Pref.) before coming to Kencho-ji. He was an outstandingly brilliant scholar-monk and was the editor of "Kencho Kokoku Zenji Hibun", Kencho-ji's official historical chronicle, which provides valuable material for research into the temple's history.

Seirai-an (Kencho-ji Tacchu)　西来庵

Official name: Seirai-an
Sect: Rinzai-Shu Kencho-ji sect
Built circa 1278 for Rankei Do-ryu Daigaku Zen-ji
Not open to the public

15 min. from JR Kita-Kamakura Sta.
Address: In Kencho-ji property

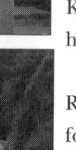

This is the Tacchu of the founder of Kencho-ji, **Rankei Do-ryu**. The temple consists of Shodo, Kaizando, Jikido and Daitetsudo (Zen meditation houses).

Behind the Kaizando, we can find the tomb of Rankei, as well as the tomb of **Mugaku Sogen**, the founder of Engaku-ji. Rankei's tombstone is oval shaped, which is the Japanese version of the Chinese style.

Dokei-in (Kencho-ji Tacchu)　同契院

Official name: Dokei-in
Sect: Rinzai-Shu Kencho-ji sect
Built by Zogai Zenkan Myogaku Zenji
Principal icon: Juichimen Kan-non Bosatsu
Not open to the public
15 min. from JR Kita-Kamakura Sta.
Address: In Kencho-ji property

Zogai Zenkan became the 31st chief priest of Kencho-ji after resigning from the post of 23rd chief priest of Engaku-ji. After he retired from Kencho-ji, he returned to Engaku-ji and built his Tacchu "Dokei-an" there. He died in 1355. Dokei-an was burnt down in 1374, and later was transferred to Kencho-ji.

Hoshu-in (Kencho-ji Tacchu)　宝珠院

Official name: Chikuon-zan Hoshu-in
Sect: Rinzai-Shu Kencho-ji sect
Inaugurated by Ryodo Soan Hongaku Zenji
Built in 1349 by Hatakeyama Kunikiyo
Principal icon: Shaka Nyorai
Not open to the public
20 min. from JR Kita-Kamakura Sta.
Address: 104 Yamanouchi, Kamakura City, Kanagawa Pref. Tel: 0467-22-2896

Ryodo Soan was the 35th chief priest of Kencho-ji. He studied Zen in Engaku-ji and served in Tosho-ji and Jufuku-ji before entering Kencho-ji. **Hatakeyama Kuniyiyo** was a general of the Ashikaga Reign, and he contibuted greatly to the establishment of the Ashikaga government.

Ryo-ho-in (Kencho-ji Tacchu)　龍峰院

Official name: Horaizan Ryu-ho-in
Sect: Rinzai-Shu Kencho-ji sect
Built in 1307 by Yakuho Tokuken Butto Kokushi
Principal icon: Sei Kan-non Bosatsu
Not open to the public
15 min. from JR Kita-Kamakura Sta.
Address: 101 Yamanouchi, Kamakura City, Kanagawa Pref. Tel: 0467-22-8734

Yakuho Tokuken was an orphan abandoned in the streets of Kamakura. Saved by monks, he served Rankei in Kencho-ji, and later became a great master in numerous Zen temples, such as Zenko-ji and Chosho-ji in Kamakura, and Nanzen-ji and Ken-nin-ji in Kyoto.

Tengen-in (Kencho-ji Tacchu)　天源院

Official name: Unkan-zan Tengen-in
Sect: Rinzai-Shu Kencho-ji sect
Built circa 1330 for Nanbo Jomin Daio Kokushi
Founded by by Hakuan Shu-i
Principal icon: Shakamuni-butsu
Not open to the public
15 min. from JR Kita-Kamakura Sta.
Address: 85 Yamanouchi, Kamakura City, Kanagawa Pref. Tel: 0467-22-2636

The 13th chief priest of Kencho-ji, **Nanbo Jomin**, first studied in China under **Rankei Do-ryu**, and later went to Kyushu for more than 30 years spreading the practice of Zen. He came back to Kamakura in 1307 to become the chief priest of Kencho-ji. He was given the title of Daio-kokushi, which was also given to numerous outstanding Zen masters.

Shoto-in (Kencho-ji Tacchu)　正統院

Official name: Tenshin-zan Shoto-in
Sect: Rinzai-Shu Kencho-ji sect
Built for Koho Ken-nichi Bukkoku Kokushi
Principal icon: Monju Bosatsu
Not open to the public
15 min. from JR Kita-Kamakura Sta.
Address: 92 Yamanouchi, Kamakura City, Kanagawa Pref. Tel: 0467-22-5207

This Tacchu was first built in Jochi-ji and then moved to its present location in 1335. **Koho Ken-nichi** (also called Bukkoku Zenji) was the 14th chief priest of Kencho-ji.

It is said that Koho Ken-nichi was once a prince under **Emperor Go-saga**, but he became a priest at the age of 16 in Kyoto before coming to Kamakura. The Shogun, **Hojo Sadatoki**, respected him greatly and made him chief priest of Jomyo-ji, Jochi-ji and Kencho-ji consecutively. He was an excellent Waka (or Tanka, 31 syllable Japanese poem) creator who wrote a book of poetry called "Bukkoku Zen-ji Waka Collection".

Kaishun-in (Kencho-ji Tacchu)　回春院

Official name: Yukoku-san Kaishun-in
Sect: Rinzai-Shu Kencho-ji sect
Built for Gyokusan Tokusen Bukkaku Zenji
Principal icon: Monju Bosatsu
20 min. from Kita-Kamakura Sta.
Address: 67 Yamanouchi, Kamakura City, Kanagawa Pref. Tel: 0467-22-6117

The 21st chief priest of Kencho-ji, **Gyokusan Tokusen (1255-1334)**, was from Shinshu (Nagano Pref.) and became a disciple of **Rankei Do-ryu** (inaugurator of Kencho-ji) in his young days. The principal icon, Monju Bosatsu is supposed to have been made in the 17th century.

The wooden statue of "Idaten" (also called Tamon-ten), made in 1659, is one of the Gods of protection. When a devil stole Buddha's ashes, Idaten chased the devil and got them back. From this legend, "Idaten" became a popularly used name for a speedy runner.

Zenkyo-in (Kencho-ji Tacchu)　禅居院

Official name: Sekibyo-zan Zenkyo-in
Sect: Rinzai-Shu Kencho-ji sect
Built between 1329-1331 for Seisetsu Seicho Daikan Zenji
Founded by Ogasawara Sadamune
Principal icon: Seikanzeon Bosatsu
Not open to the public
15 min. from JR Kita-Kamakura Sta.
Address: 1534 Yamanouchi, Kamakura City, Kanagawa Pref. Tel: 0467-22-7974

The 22nd chief priest of Kencho-ji, **Seisetsu Seicho**, came from China to Japan in 1326 by invitation of **Hojo Takatoki**, the 15th Shogun of the Kamakura Reign. He successively served in the chief post in Jochi-ji and Engaku-ji, and in Ken-nin-ji and Nanzen-ji in Kyoto, as well as founding Kanzen-ji in Shinano county (Nagano Prefecture). He was an excellent poet who wrote a book "Zenkyo-Shu" (Zen Buddhist collection).

The temple has a secret statue, "Marishi-ten", which is an animistic icon of fire in popular Indian belief. This God was worshiped widely by warriors in Japan as a protector from flood, fires or wars. According to the manuscript kept in the temple, the Emperor of China entrusted the statue to Seisetsu Seicho when he was leaving the country for Japan.

En-no-ji (Kencho-ji Tacchu)　円応寺

Official name: Arai-zan En-no-ji
Sect: Rinzai-Shu Kencho-ji sect
Built by Chigaku Zenji in 1250
Principal icon: Enma-O
Open 9:00-16:00 (spring and summer) 9:00-13:30 (winter)
Entrance fee: ¥200

15 min. from JR Kita-Kamakura Sta.
Address: 1543 Yamanouchi, Kamakura City, Kanagawa Pref. Tel: 0467-25-1095

It is said that En-no-ji was originally in the Hase area (near the Great Buddha), but had to move to the present location because of tsunami damage in 1703.

This temple may be the most scary temple in Kamakura. The temple worships "Ju-O" the ten infernal judge Gods.

The principal icon "Enma-Daio" is the work of the great sculptor of the Kamakura era, **Unkei** and designated as a national cultural asset. Enma-O usually looks scary with his eyes and mouth wide open, but this one looks as if he is laughing. For that reason, Enma-O of En-no-ji has long been popularly called "Warai Enma" (Laughing Enma).

Enma Daio, as the ruling judge, brings in a verdict five weeks after one's death hearing the reports made by his four assistant kings. Thereby, the defendants are ordered to go to one of the Six Stages of the World: Hell (Jigoku), World of Hungry Devil (Gaki), Realm of Beasts (Chikusho), World of Fury (Ashura), Human Being (Ningen) and Heaven (Gokuraku). Henjo-O decides specifically which one of the Six Worlds the defendants will be sentenced to. The world of Human Beings, for example, has various types; wealthy or poor, peaceful or violent, beautiful or ugly, strong or weak and so on. Taizan-O gives personal conditions such as span of life and sex, etc..

The sculptor **Unkei** made also the famous pair of "Nio" of Todai-ji in Nara. In his last years, he fell seriously ill and was almost on the point of death. On the middle way to another world, he went through the judgement barriers by "Ju-O" (the ten infernal judge Gods) and arrived at the ruling judge, Enma Daio. He then was interrogated.

"You are Unkei, are'nt you? In the human world, they say that I am too harsh and merciless. But, it's not true. I am the judge who watches people's behavior during their life time. Justice is my cause, so to speak. Look at my features very carefully. I'll send you back home again if you promise to sculpt my true aspect in order to show it to all human beings."

According to the legend, Unkei answered "yes", and was revived. Using his clear memory of the infernal world, he create a huge 1.9 m high, ruddy-faced terrible, demonish figure.

(3) North-east Area

<Nikaido and Juniso>

MODEL COURSE (A)	MODEL COURSE (B)	MODEL COURSE (C)
JR Kamakura Sta. ↓ 5min.by bus or 20min. by walking Egara Tenjin-sha shrine ↓ 5min.walking Kamakura-gu(oto-no-miya)shrine ↓ 10min.walking Zuisen-ji or Kakuon-ji	JJR Kamakura Sta ↓ 10min.by bus Sugimoto-dera ↓ 10min.walking Hokoku-ji ↓ 5min.walking Jomyo-ji ↓ 1min. Kumano-Jinja ↓ 15min.walking Myo-o-in ↓ 10min.walking Kosoku-ji ↓ 15min.walking Juniso Jinja	JR Kamakura Sta. ↓ 5min.by bus or 20min. by walking Egara Tenjin-sha shrine ↓ 5min.walking Kamakura-gu(oto-no-miya)shrine ↓ 10min.walking Zuisen-ji & Kakuon-ji ↓ 20min.walking back to wakaremichi bus stop ↓ 5min.by bus Sugimoto-dera ↓ 10min.walking Hokoku-ji ↓ 5min.walking Jomyo-ji ↓ 1min. Kumano-Jinja ↓ 15min.walking Myo-o-in ↓ 10min.walking Kosoku-ji ↓ 15min.walking Juniso Jinja

Egara Tenjin-sha 荏柄天神社

Official name: Egara Tenjin-sha
Enshrined God: Deity of Scholarship
Founded in 1104
Distinctive property: Academic achievements
Annual festival: July 20,25
Sub shrine: Kumano-sha
Open: 7:30-18:30
20 min. from JR Kamakura Sta. or 5 min. from Wakaremichi bus stop.
Take a bus bound for Oto-no-miya (No.20) from JR Kamakura Sta. east exit
Address: 74 Nikaido, Kamakura, Kanagawa, Tel: 0467-25-1772

Tenjin shrines are dedicated to the spirit of **Sugawara Michizane**, a Heian period politician and scholar. Tenjin-sama are particularly popular among students preparing for entrance exams. These shrines can be recognized by statues of oxen, and plum trees, Michizane's favorite tree.

Legend has it that on August 25, 1104, the spirit of Tenjin descended at this site, and local people constructed a small shrine dedicated to the spirit of Michizane, who had for centuries been venerated as a patron deity of scholarship.

Sugawara Michizane was born in Kyoto of noble birth. Not only did he become a good politician, but also a great scholar and calligrapher. With his talent, he was promoted quickly to the highest ranking minister. An aristocrat, **Fujiwara Tokihira**, jealous of Michizane's success, successfully arranged to have him expelled. Two years later Michizane died in sorrow at Dazaifu in Kyushu.

After Michizane's death, a series of thunderbolts fell on Kyoto, one of them directly striking the living quarters of the emperor. In addition, members of the Fujiwara family, including Tokihira himself, died mysteriously one after another. These disasters instigated the construction of shrines all over Japan to calm Michizane's tortured soul.

Because the shrine is home to the deity of scholarship, it became popular as a pilgrimage for academic hopefuls. In early spring, students preparing for entrance exams flock here to offer prayers for success. They buy a wooden tablet with a picture called "ema" and inscribe their wishes on the back. These ema are

Brush Monument

Gingko tree

offered to Tenjin, and are strung around the shrine for all to see.

Egara Tenjin is one of the top three Tenjin shrines in Japan. The other two are Dazaifu Tenman-gu, where Sugawara Michizane was exiled, and Kitano Tenman-gu in Kyoto, Michizane's birthplace.

On the left-hand side of the main hall lies an egg-shaped stone called **Kappa Fudezuka**, which was installed in 1971. Kappa is an imaginary animal, which lives in the water and has a shell on his back and a dish on top of his head. The monument shows a kappa as sketched by the famous cartoonist, **Shimizu Kon (1912-1974)**. On the back of the stone, the words "Kappa Fudezuka" are engraved. The original calligraphy is by **Kawabata Yasunari**, the Nobel Prize winning author.

Behind the Kappa Fudezuka, there is a tall bronze brush-shaped monument, erected in 1989. On all sides of the monument, we can admire 154 different kappa profiles, all donated by cartoonists in praise of Shimizu's achievements.

On the right of the shrine grounds, there is a sacred Gingko tree. It is roughly 900 years old and its girth measures 6.5m the second largest one in Kamakura after the one in Tsurugaoka Hachiman-gu Shrine.

Ema

Ema are wooden plates on which prayers or petitions are written and used as votive tablets. Normally, a horse is drawn on the tablet (hence the name "e" picture and "ma" horse). After writing a wish or two, such as success in an entrance examination or a happy marriage, petitioners hang them at the doors of the shrine and pray that their wishes will be answered.

Kamakura-gu 鎌倉宮

Official name: Kamakura-gu or Oto-no-miya or Daito-no-miya Founded by Emperor Meiji in 1869
Enshrined Gods: Oto-no Miya Morinaga Shin-no
Distinctive property: Peace and happiness
Annual festival: August 20
Sub shrines: Sessha, Minamino-Kata-sha, Murakami-sha
Last stop for bus bound for Oto-no-miya (No.20)
5 min. from JR Kamakura Sta. east exit
Address: 154 Nikaido, Kamakura City, Kanagawa Pref. Tel: 0467-22-0318

Kamakura-gu Shrine is considerably new, having been erected to the spirit of **Prince Morinaga (1308-1335)** in 1870 by **Emperor Meiji**. Prince Morinaga is said to be the third child of **Emperor Godaigo (1288-1339)**. As Emperor Godaigo had many court ladies who gave birth to 36 children, when the Prince was born is not clear. The The Shrine's alias is Oto-no-miya after the Prince's full name, Oto-no-miya Morinaga Shinno.

In 1333, the Kamakura Shogunate ended and the ruling power was temporalily handed over to Emperor Godaigo, restoring the sovereignty of Japan to the Imperial Court. **Ashikaga Takauji (1305-1358)**, the founder of the Ashikaga Shogunate, helped the Emperor win the battle against the Hojos in Kamakura. However, once he succeeded in beating the Hojos, he betrayed the Emperor and captured Prince Morinaga. Prince Morinaga was sent to Kamakura, where he was kept under house-arrest at Toko-ji, a Zen temple located at the present Kamakura-gu site.

In 1335, Takauji's younger brother, **Ashikaga Tadayoshi (1306-1352)**, who was in Kamakura to defend the city, was attacked by the Hojos. When he saw that he was unable to save the prince from the enemy, he decided to kill him. Prince Morinaga died at the age of 26.

The site of the Shrine had formerly been owned by Tokei-ji temple. When Prince Morinaga was

Dungeon of Prince Morinaga

killed, one of his sisters entered Tokei-ji as a nun to console her brother's soul. When Emperor Meiji ordered this shrine built in 1870, Tokei-ji offered this property due to this historical connection.

A court-lady named **Minami-no-kata**, who served Prince Morinaga, was pregnant with his baby boy at the time the prince was killed. The son later became a monk of Nichiren-shu sect with the name of **Nichiei**. He eventually founded Myoho-ji, and built his parents' cenotaphs in the temple. On the hill top of Myoho-ji courtyard, one can find the prince's tomb.

Right behind the Honden is a dungeon where Prince Morinaga was reportedly held in captivity for nine months. However, in fact, he was not imprisoned in this dungeon, but was kept under house arrest instead.

Takigi-Noh performance

In the courtyard of Kamakura-gu, every October 8 and 9 Noh, drama is performed from 19:00 to 21:00. This event is called "Takigi (burning firewood) Noh", with only small bonfires for lighting. Tickets to the performances are available by contacting the Kamakura Tourist Association.

Omamori

Omamori are Japanese amulets dedicated to particular Shinto deities as well as Buddhist figures. They contain papers or pieces of wood with canon or sutra written on them, and are supposed to bring good luck to the bearer on particular occasions, tasks or ordeals. Most of them cover a single area such as health, love, or studies.

Omamori are also used to ward off bad luck and are often spotted on bags, in cars, etc. for saftey in travel. Many omamori are specific in design to the shrines or temples where they were made. Omamori should never be opened or they lose their protective capacities.

Omikuji

Omikuji are fortune telling slips of paper found at many shrines and temples. We randomly choose a paper, or draw a numbered stick from a hole in a box, show it to a monk or clerk, and a corresponding Omikuji slip is given. They contain predictions ranging from daikichi ("extreme good luck") to daikyo ("extreme bad luck").

When people are not pleased with what they draw, such as getting "Kyo" or worse, they return it to the shrine by tying the Omikuji paper around a tree branch and try again at a later date.

However, Omikuji was originally not a fortune telling system. It was a ritual ceremony in order to guess a god's true intention, and a kind of sorcery for making a difficult decision. They would place pieces of paper on which various choices were written in three directions, and wave a wand (with hemp and paper streamers) over them. The paper that would fly up would be chosen as the solution. This way of decision making was used also for the selection of community chief or for giving a name to new born babies.

Zuisen-ji 瑞泉寺

Official name: Kinpei-zan Zuisen-ji
Sect: Rinzai-Shu Engaku-ji sect
Built in 1327
Opened by Muso Soseki
Principal icon (Hon-zon): Shaka Muni-butsu
Open 9:00-17:00
Entrance fee: ¥100
10 min. from Oto-no-miya stop on the bus bound for Oto-no-miya (No.20) from JR Kamakura Sta. east exit
Address: 710 Nikai-do, Kamakura City, Kanagawa Pref. Tel: 0467-22-1191

Kaizan-do

Garden by Muso Soseki

A 10 minute walk takes you to the gate standing as if it were the end of the road. The main gate is always closed to the public, so one has to get into the temple through the path on the side. There are two different slopes to choose from; the gentle one on the right called Onna Zaka (slope for women) and the steep one, Otoko Zaka (slope for men). Onna Zaka leads to the San-mon gate and Otoko Zaka to the rock garden.

Zuisen-ji's origin was a hut for practicing Zen which **Muso Soseki** built in 1327, just five years before the collapse of the Kamakura Shogunate. Muso was also a garden designer of the time and very well known for designing the gardens of Saiho-ji and Tenryu-ji in Kyoto.

Many Zen Buddhist monks of different temples in Kamakura used this temple for their poetry club gatherings.

After the Kamakura Shogunate collapsed, the Ashikaga family ruled over Kamakura, and the 1st Ashikaga commander, **Ashikaga Motouji**, became a disciple of Muso and named the temple Zuisen-ji.

The most characteristc feature of the garden is the carved rock caves.

Tsurube-no-I <10 Famous Wells of Kamakura>

Deep at the back of Zuisen-ji temple, there is a Jizo-do Hall. On the right side of the hall, we can find Tsurube (bucket) well. It may be called this because this is the only well that is equipped with a bucket.

Kakuon-ji 覚園寺

Official name: Jubu-sen Shingon-in Kakuon-ji
Sect: Old Shingon-Shu Sen-nyu-ji-sect
Opened by Chikai Shin-e
Built by Hojo Sadatoki in 1296
Principal icon (Hon-zon): Yakushi Nyorai
Open 10:00-15:00(guidance every hour, except 12:00 on week days)
Closed on April 27, Month of August, from December 21 to January 7, rainy days, stormy days.
Entrance fee: ¥300
Take a bus bound for Oto-no-miya (No.20) from JR Kamakura Sta. east exit, get off at Oto-no-miya bus stop and walk 10 min.
Address: 421 Nikaido, Kamakura City, Kanagawa Pref. Tel: 0467-22-1195

Main gate

Turning to the left from Kamakura-gu gate, follow the narrow road uphill deep into Yakushi-do-gayatsu for about 10 minutes. Here you will find Kakuon-ji, one of Kamakura connoisseurs' favorite spots.

In 1218, the 2nd Kamakura Shogun, **Hojo Yoshitoki**, built a small altar house, Okura Yakushi-do, where he prayed for a stop to the Mongolian invasions. In 1296, it was promoted to a temple, but the original thatched roofed Yakushi-do still remains.

The monks regularly guide visitors around the temple every hour for 50 minutes. There are three important buildings to see; Aizen-do, Jizo-do and the

Yakushi-do. The first is Aizen-do, where three Gods of esoteric Buddhism, Aizen Myo-o, Fudo Myo-o and Ashuku Nyorai are kept. Myo-o is a typical Esoteric God with an expression of wrath. Myo-o strongly admonishes those disobedient to Buddha's teaching. The esoteric Buddhism here is a more closed and secret Buddhism, similar to that current in Tibet. It was introduced to Japan by Saicho and Kukai from China in the 9th century. The former established Tendai-shu and the latter Shingon-shu. Kakuon-ji is a Shingon-Shu temple, which is rare in Kamakura.

Aizen Myo-o is a God of love, although he has an expression of wrath. He can convert love and passion to Satori (spiritual awakening). Couples with troubles would come here and pray for the recovery of their relationship.

In Jizo-do, the famous Kuro-Jizo (Black Jizo) is worshipped. His entirely black body signifies that he is in eternal pain from being burnt, sacrificing himself for dead sinners.

Kuro-Jizo is not painted black. It has been cleaned many times, but the wood turned black in time. On August 8 every year, at midnight, many people come to worship Kuro-Jizo in the "Kurayami-mairi" (worshipper in the dark).

Under the thatched roof of the ancient Japanese style wooden house, Yakushi-do, we find the Yakushi Sanzon, the three Yakushi Gods, made of strong, Japanese apricot wood. These are Yakushi Nyorai, Nikko Bosatsu (Bosatsu of sunlight) and Gakko Bosatsu (Bosatsu of moonlight). On both sides facing each other, the 6 armed Guard Gods, 12 in all, are posed in different positions. As the 12 Gods represent the 12 animals of the Chinese calender, each God has a rat, cow, tiger, rabbit, dragon etc. on its head.

Also in the Yakushi-do, the statue of Amida Nyorai is something not to miss. It's called "Tako Amida" (tako means octopus). This Amida statue holds another Buddha in its belly, and that Buddha's posture looks like an octopus in its pot.

On the ceiling of Yakushi-do, there is a big painting of a dragon and a wood panel beside the painting. This very plate was signed by **Ashikaga Takauji**, the 1st Shogun of the Muromachi Reign, at the occasion of the restoration of Yakushi-do in 1354.

Munetate-no-I <10 Famous Wells of Kamakura>

This well is behind the Yakushi-do of Kakuon-ji temple, but not open to the public. One can visit inside Kakuon-ji temple by the guidance of the temple's monk but no photographes are allowed.

Sugimoto-dera 杉本寺

Official name: Daizo-zan Kan-non-in Sugimoto-dera
Sect: Tendai-Shu
Built in 734
Opened by Gyoki Bosatsu
Founded by Komyo Kogo (Empress)
Principal icon (Hon-zon): Juichimen Kan-non (eleven faced Kan-non)
Open 8:00-16:30
Entrance fee: ¥200 (adult) & ¥100 (children)
1 min. from Sugimoto Kan-non bus stop by bus bound for Kanazawa Hakkei (No.24) or Tachiarai (No.23), or Highland Circular line (No.20) from JR Kamakura Sta. east exit
Address: 903 Nikai-do, Kamakura City, Kanagawa Pref. Tel: 0467-22-3463

Moss covered steps

Sugimoto-dera is the oldest temple in Kamakura, having been built 450 years before the Kamakura Shogunate was established. The founder Gyoki was one of the greatest monks of early Buddhism in Japan. He contributed very much to liberating Buddhism from being a restrictive, authoritarian religion to a popular and social welfare oriented faith. People greatly admired him for his devoted works of irrigation and bridge constructions, which relieved tax-burdened peasants and developed the rice agriculture. They used to call him Gyoki Bosatsu which meant the incarnation of Buddha.

Gyoki first came to Kamakura when he was traveling around Japan in order to petition for money for the Great Buddha's construction in Nara.

Sugimoto-dera is on the way to the Juniso area, just beside the "Kanazawa Kaido" road. It has a narrow, steep, moss covered stairway and up at the main gate, there are two Ni-O guard statues.

In the Hon-do, we can see three Juichimen Kan-non. The one on the left is the oldest and is said to have been made by Gyoki himself. The one in the center was

Nio by Unkei

86

made in 851 by the monk Jikaku Daishi, and the one on the right in 985 by the monk Eshin Sozu. The Jizo Bosatsu made by Unkei, the famous sculptor, and Bishamonten made by Takuma Hogan, are in the Hon-do, which is covered by a thatched roof. It is certain that visitors here feel a difference from other Kamakura temples, something of the older, more primordial period of early Buddhism in Japan, such as we find in Nara.

The name Sugimoto derives from a legend that in November, 1189, the Hondo was razed by fire. However, the three Juichimen Kan-non escaped from the fire and waited for help hiding under the big cedar tree in the garden. Cedar tree is called "Sugi" in Japanese and "Sugi no Moto" means "under the tree". This tale is written in "Azuma Kagami", the old historical chronicle of Japan.

About Kan-non

Senju Kan-non is an icon of various Kan-non Bosatsu. Nyorai or Amida Nyorai is the master God of Heaven, and his two assistant-like Gods are on both his sides. They are Bosatsu; Seiji Bosatsu and Kan-non Bosatsu. Kan-non, also called Kan-Jizai-Bosatsu or Kanzeon Bosatsu, is a God who saves human beings by changing his features freely in the most effective way. Kan-non could become Juichimen (eleven faced) Kan-non or Senju (thousand handed) Kan-non. The former has 11 faces on the head. The three in front are peaceful Bosatsu faces, three faces of wrath are on the left and three smiling ones on the right. The one on the back is laughing. Adding its own face or sometimes Nyorai face on the top of head to these ten faces, we form the eleven faced Kan-non.

Senju Kan-non should be correctly called "Senju Sengan Kan-Jizai-Bosatsu", meaning "Thousand hands and eyes Omnipotent Bosatsu".

This divine power of a thousand hands is expressed and formed in numerical and mathematical logic in Buddhist icon making. More generally, the 11 faced Kan-non would be the base. It is said that each hand of Kan-non saves 25 people. The calculation goes that if 10 of them join their 40 hands, then 25 multiplied by 40, or 1,000, people could be saved.

Hokoku-ji　報国寺

Official name: Koshin-zan Hokoku-ji
Sect: Rinzai-Shu Kencho-ji sect
Built in 1334
Opened by Tengan Eko
Founded by Ashikaga Ietoki
Principal icon (Hon-zon): Shaka Nyorai
Open 9:00-16:00

Entrance fee: ¥200 (adult) ¥100 (infant)
3 min. from Jomyo-ji bus stop. Take a bus bound for Kanazawa Hakkei (No.24) or Tachiarai (No.23), or Highland Circular line (No.36) from JR Kamakura Sta. east exit
Address: 2-7-4 Jomyo-ji, Kamakura City, Kanagawa Pref. Tel: 0467-22-0762

Bamboo garden

This temple is so famous for its bamboo garden that it is popularly called Take-dera. ("Take" means bamboo.) It was built in 1334 at the beginning of the Ashikaga reign by the father of Ashikaga Takauji, the first Shogun of the Muromachi Shogunate. (The Muromachi Shogunate set its capital in Kyoto, and Kamakura was ruled by the Ashikaga commanders.)

This temple's property reaches for 5 kilometers south as far as Mt. Kinuhari (120m high).

Visitors can enjoy green tea and Japanese sweets in front of the bamboo garden, or stroll through the many gardens on the temple grounds. The Sunday Zen meditation course welcomes beginners.

Jomyo-ji 浄妙寺

Official name: Toka-san Jomyo-ji
Sect: Rinzai-Shu Kencho-ji sect
Opened by Taiko Gyoyu in 1188
Founded by Ashikaga Yoshikane
Principal icon (Hon-zon): Shaka Nyorai
Open 9:00-16:30
Entrance fee: ¥100
2 min. from Jomyo-ji stop on the bus bound for Kanazawa Hakkei (No.24) or Tachiarai (No.23), or the Highland Circular line (No.36) from JR Kamakura Sta. east exit
Address: 3-8-31 Jomyo-ji, Kamakura City, Kanagawa Pref. Tel: 0467-22-2818

San-mon

Jomyo-ji is an old temple ranked 5th of the five great temples in Kamakura. **Ashikaga Yoshi-**

Kisen-an garden

Kamatari Inari Shrine

kane, a high ranking minister under Minamoto Yoritomo, founded an esoteric Buddhist temple called Gokuraku-ji, inviting the esoteric monk, **Taiko Gyoyu**, to be the 1st master. Ten years later, Gyoyu met the Zen Buddhist master **Eisai** and learned Rinzai Zen Buddhism from him. **Minamoto Yoritomo**, his wife **Hojo Masako** and their son **Minamoto Sanetomo** all became his devout disciples. Later, around 1258, the priest **Geppo Ryonen** of Kencho-ji took over the temple and changed the name to Jomyo-ji, and at the same time the temple was converted to Zen Buddhism. Subsequently, several highly distinguished priests succeeded the mastership, and toward the 14th century it became one of the most important temples in Kamakura.

The temple's property is designated a National Historic site. The Hon-do is covered by a simply designed copper roof.

On the left hand side of the Hon-do, a tea ceremony house, Kisen-an welcomes guests. Visitors can attend tea ceremony while contemplating the Zen style Japanese rock garden (Karezansui).

On the right hand side of the temple, there is a path that leads to Kamatari Inari Jinja, a Shinto shrine. **Fujiwara Kamatari** was a politician in 7th century Japan, who led the Taika-no-Kaishin (political restoration of Taika in 645). When he passed by this area on the way to Kashima Shrine in Ibaragi Pref., in his dream, he was told by an old man to bury a spear with a sickle head in this land. Next day, a white fox appeared and led him up to the mountain. Kamatari did what he was told in the dream and built a small shrine there. It is also said that the name Kamakura originates from this legend.

Kumano Jinja 熊野神社

Official name: Kumano Jinja
Enshrined Gods: Izanagi-no-Mikoto, Izanami-no-Mikoto, Ameno-Uzume-no-Kami
Distinctive property: Prosperity and fertility
Annual festival: Closest holiday to July 17
5 min. from Jomyo-ji bus stop. Take a bus bound for

Tachiarai (No.23) from JR Kamakura Sta. east exit
Address: 64 Jomyo-ji, Kamakura City, Kanagawa Pref.

This is the "Chinju" (main village shrine) of the Jomyo-ji area. The founding date is not known, but, we know that it was reconstructed between 1394-1428 and again between 1504-1521. In 1873, it was promoted to Chinju of the area.

It is said that the residence of **Ashikaga Naoyoshi**, the younger brother of **Ashikaga Takauji** (the 1st Shogun of the Muromachi Reign), was built on land to the east of the shrine,.

"Kumano" is a very popular name for shrines. There are three thousand shrines named "Kumano" in the country, all originating from the three Kumano shrines in Wakayama Prefecture. The Kumano region was regarded a sacred area where monks have practiced ascetic discipline since the 8th century.

Myo-o-in 明王院

Official name: Hansei-zan Kanki-ji Myo-o-in
Sect: Shingon-Shu Omuro sect
Built in 1235
Opened by Tengan Eko
Founded by Fujiwara Yoritsune
Principal icon (Hon-zon): Fudo Myo-o
Open hours not specified
4 min. from Sensui Bashi bus stop. Take a bus bound for Kanazawa Hakkei (No.24) or Tachiarai (No.23) from JR Kamakura Sta. east exit
Address: 32 Juniso, Kamakura City, Kanagawa Pref. Tel: 0467-25-0416

After **Minamoto Sanetomo** was assasinated in 1219 at Tsurugaoka Hachiman-gu Shrine, **Minamoto Yoritsune** succeeded the Kamakura Shogunate. It was found that the Juniso area was one of Kamakura's Kimon (in Buddhism, Kimon is the direction from which devils or disasters come), so Yoritsune built a Myo-o hall here in order to protect the capital.

Myo-o of Myo-o-in is a typical Buddhist Esoteric God with an expression of wrath. It is said that Myo-o is another aspect of Nyorai, the God of Tenderness. Likewise, Dainichi Nyorai may become Fudo Myo-o and Amida Nyorai to Dai-

Itoku-Myo-o. (But, this concept is found in Esoteric Buddhism, not in Zen Buddhism nor in Jodo-shu or other denominations.) There are 5 Myo-o Gods; Fudo Myo-o, Go-sanze Myo-o, Gundari Myo-o, Dai-Itoku Myo-o, and Kongo Yasha Myo-o. They are Gods who teach us what we should do not by smiles but by fear.

Before reaching the temple, there is a bridge called Futatsu-bashi. The two big rocks that can be found below the bridge were the corner stones of the temple at its beginning. The Hon-do has a thatched roof, and old style architecture.

Kosoku-ji 光触寺

Official name: Ganzo-zan Kosoku-ji
Sect: Ji-Shu
Built in 1279
Opened by Sakua
Principal icon (Hon-zon): Amida Sanzon
Open 10:00-16:00
Admission free, to see Amida Sanzon ¥300 (more than 10 people necessary)
2 min. from Juniso bus stop. Take a bus bound for Kanazawa Hakkei (No.24) or Tachiarai (No.23) from JR Kamakura Sta. east exit.
Address: 793 Juniso, Kamakura City, Kanagawa Pref.
Tel: 0467-22-6864

Ippen

If we follow the Namerikawa river to the Northeast from central Kamakura, we enter the Juniso Area, where we can find some beautiful temples. Kosoku-ji is the remotest among them. Ji-Shu denomination was established by the **Master Ippen**, who was an itinerant monk. He used to chant Nenbutsu sutra "Namu Amida Butsu" and tried to make people worship Amida. His main temple is Yugyo-ji in Fujisawa.

Entering the temple's gate, which is always open, there is a graveyard on both sides of the walkway.

The Hon-zon, Amida Sanzon, is called "Hohoyake Amida" (Burnt Cheek Amida). This nickname comes from the following legend.

Once upon a time, a lady called **Machi-no-Tsubone**, who used to serve Minamoto Yoritomo, donated this statue to the temple. One day, something was stolen and a monk named **Manzai Hoshi**, who was serving the lady in the house,

Shio-name Jizo

became the suspect. He was punished and branded on his cheek. But surprisingly, next day there was no trace on his cheek. They therefore branded him again. That night in Machi-no-Tsubone's dream, Amida Nyorai asked her.

"Why do you brand me on the cheek?"

Machi-no-Tsubone immediately went to the temple to see Amida and found the burnt trace on the cheek. She of course pardoned the monk but the trace never disappeared after that.

On the right hand side of the Hon-do, there is a small hut, containing one bigger Jizo and five smaller Jizo statues, six in all. They are called "Shio-name Jizo" (Jizo who licks salt). In old times, the route through Juniso led to Mutsu-ura port. One day, a salt marchant of Mutsu-ura donated his salt to the Jizo on his way to Kamakura in the morning. When he passed by again on the way back in the evening, the salt was gone. Ever since, people have been offring salt to Jizo.

Roku-Jizo

Rokujizo on Yuigahama St.

A row of six stone statues of Jizo can be found in many temples in Kamakura. They are called "Roku Jizo" (Six Jizo) and each Jizo is assigned to one of the Six Stages of afterlife to save wandering souls.

In Buddhism, it is believed that once we die, we will all be finally classified into one of the following six "Kai" (world or stage), Jigoku (hell), Gaki (hungry devil), Chikusho (beasts), Ashura (a scene of bloodshed), Ningen (human beings) and Tenjo (heaven). Unless the dead person is classified as fit for heaven, he or she will be sent back to this painful world again, or in the worst case, to Hell.

Six Jizo, therefore, with each one assigned to one of the six stages, rescue those in distress from the stage they are in. The most famous Roku-Jizo is the one standing about 500 meters southwest of Geba crossing, on the roadside of Yuigahama street, leading to Hase Kan-non and the Great Buddha. Also, most temples have Roku-Jizo within their grounds. Jizo is a symbol of hope, so to speak, so it is never too late to pray for salvation.

Juniso-Jinja　十二社神社

Official name: Juniso Jinja
Enshrined Gods: Amatsu-kami-Nanahashira, Kunitsu-kami-Itsuhashira
Founded in 1278
Distinctive property: Prosperity and fecundity
Annual festival: Closest Sunday to September 9
Sub-shrines: Yamano Kami, Hosojin, Usa Hachiman, Jinushi Kami

1 min. from Juniso Jinja stop on the bus bound for Tachiarai (No.23) from JR Kamakura Sta. east exit
Address: 285 Juniso, Kamakura City, Kanagawa Pref.

This shrine was called Kumano Juniso Gongen-sha in old times and was situated in the courtyard of Kosoku-ji temple until it was moved to the present location in 1838. At the Meiji Restoration, the shrine's name was changed to the present one and it became "Chinju" of Juniso village.

Beside the Tori-i gate, a heavy stone called "Hyakkan-ishi" is located. Hyakkan (100 kan) is equivalent to 375kg, but in fact this stone weighs 112kg. In old times, at the occasion of festivals, local men used to compete by lifting this stone.

(4) North-West Area

<Sasuke and Ogigayatsu>

MODEL COURSE (A)	MODEL COURSE (B)
JR Kamakura Sta.	JR Kamakura Sta.
↓10min.	↓25min.
Tatsumi Shrine	Zeniarai Benten
↓1min.	↓5min.
Yasaka Daijin Shrine	Sasuke Inari Shrine
↓0min.	↓20min.
Jufuku-ji	Tatsumi Shrine
↓5min.	↓1min.
Eisho-ji	Yasaka Shrine
↓10min.	↓0min.
Kaizo-ji	Jufuku-ji
↓15min.	↓5min.
Joko-Myo-ji	Eisho-ji
↓5min.	↓10min.
Yakuo-ji	Kaizo-ji
↓25min.	↓15min.
Sasuke Inari Shrine	Joko-Myo-ji
↓5min.	↓5min.
Zeniarai benten	Yakuo-ji (all by walking)
↓15min..	
Kuzuharaoka Shrine (all by walking)	

North-West

Tatsumi Jinja 巽神社

Official name: Tatsumi Jinja
Enshrined Gods: Okitsu-Hikono-Kami, Okitsu-Hime-no-Kami, Homusubi-no-Kami
Built by Sakanoueno-Tamuramaro in 801
Distinctive property: Protection against fire
Annual festival: November 28
Sub shrine: Suwa-sha
10 min. from JR Kamakura Sta. west exit
Address: 1-9-7 Ogi-gayatsu, Kamakura City, Kanagawa Pref.

This is a very old shrine that was originally built in Kuzuharaoka by **General Sakanoueno-Tamuramaro**, who conquered the indigenous Ezo tribe (supposedly Ainu) in northern Japan in the 9th century. Later in 1049, **Minamoto Yoriyoshi**, who built the Moto Hachiman shrine, remodeled the shrine building and moved it to the present location near Jufuku-ji temple as the Chinju God of Jufuku-ji. The pair of stone lanterns flanking the shrine's main hall was originally in Tsurugaoka Hachiman-gu. As it is south-east of Jufuku-ji temple, the shrine was named "Tatsumi" (south-east direction in oriental folklore).

Yasaka Daijin 八坂大神

Official name: Yasaka Daijin or Soma Ten-no
Enshrined Gods: Susano-no-Mikoto, Emperor Kanmu, Prince Kuzuhara, Takamochi-o
Built by Soma Jiro Morotsune in 1192
Distinctive property: Protection from epidemic disease, agriculture, commerce
Annual festival: July 12
Sub shrine: Ne-no-Jinja
10 min. from JR Kamakura Sta. west exit
Address: 1-13-45 Ogi-gayatsu, Kamakura City, Kanagawa Pref.

This chinju (local shrine) of Ogi-gayatsu area is otherwise called "Soma Ten-no" because it was originally a temple-shrine that **Soma Jiro Morotsune**, the son of **Chiba Tsunetane** (Yoritomo's vassal), built for his tutelary deity in 1192 near Tatsumi Jinja. He was an excellent warrior who contributed to Yoritomo's army in the battles against the Fujiwara clan in northern Japan in 1189. He also was so religious that he became a devout ascetic of Nenbutsu Buddhism (the origin of Jodo-shu).

The shrine was later moved twice, the first time into a yagura (cave) near Jokomyo-ji Temple, and the second time to a spot near Jufuku-ji, before settling down in the present location just next to Jufuku-ji temple. The shrine's original name was changed to Yasaka Daijin at the Meiji Restoration.

Jufuku-ji 寿福寺

Official name: Kikoku-zan Jufuku-Kongo-Zen-ji
Sect: Rinzai-Shu Kencho-ji sect
Inaugurated by Eisai in 1200
Built by Hojo Masako
Principal icon (Hon-zon): Hokan Shaka Nyorai
Always open, but only to the second gate
10 min. from JR Kamakura Sta. west exit
Address: 1-17-7 Ogi-gayatsu, Kamakura City, Kanagawa Pref. Tel:0467-22-6607

Jufuku-ji is ranked 3rd of the 5 Great Temples in Kamakura. The inaugurator **Eisai** is the priest who introduced Rinzai Zen Buddhism into Japan from China. The temple was erected almost half-a-century earlier than Kencho-ji was, and yet it ranks third on the list of the Five Great Zen Temples in Kamakura, since Zen was not its denomination at the very beginning.

Eisai was born in Okayama Prefecture and took Buddhist vows at the age of 14. First, he entered Enryaku-ji near Kyoto, the center of the Tendai-shu sect, and then visited China twice, in 1168 and in 1178. Eisai is also known for introducing "tea" from China. He brought tea seedlings into Japan, and wrote a book on the medical effects of tea. Tea ceremony culture originates from Kamakura Zen Buddhism.

The book written by Eisai himself is designated as a National Cultural Asset and kept in the Kamakura Treasure Museum.

The founder, **Hojo Masako,** erected the temple to propitiate the soul of her departed husband, **Minamoto Yoritomo**, following his sudden death in 1199.

The present main hall was rebuilt between 1751 and 1763. The principal icon (Hon-zon), Hokan Shaka Nyorai, is a 282cm (9.4ft.) high statue with his two attendants, Fugen Bosatsu on the right and Monju Bosatsu on the left. It is enshrined in the main hall. but can only be seen on special occasions.

This Shaka is crowned and called Kago Shaka. (Kago means a basket). It was named after its statue making tecnique. The figure was formed with clay over a wooden frame. Then, forms and lines were made by sticking on multiple layers of hemp cloth with lacquer. When it dried, the frame and the clay base were taken out. The statue stays empty inside like a basket. It is said to be made in 1395, but nobody knows who the artist was.

Behind the main building is the temple's graveyard, which is open to the public. We can go in from the left-hand path of the inner gate or through a narrow street before arriving at the temple. Below the cliff wall on the back of the graveyard, there is a row of yagura caves where the gorinto, or five-tier-stone stupa, of **Hojo Masako** and her son, **Minamoto Sanetomo** are placed. Record shows that their ashes were buried at Choshoju-in temple, which no longer exists.

According to historians, the gorinto here represents a typical style made in the second half of the Kamakura era, and therefore, these are not real tombs but cenotaphs erected for the repose of the departed.

The Ogi-gayatsu area where the temple is situated is where **Minamoto Yoshitomo**, the father of Kamakura's 1st shogun, Minamoto Yoritomo lived. Therefore, the mountain in the back, has the name "Genji-yama" which means "Mountain of the Minamoto Family".

Yagura

Takatoki Yagura

Yagura are caves where cremated remains of samurai or priests are buried. In 1242, the Kamakura Shogunate forbade the construction of large graveyards as flat land space was scarce. Tombs of the high ranking people therefore, were built in caves in hillside cliffs. It is said there are no less than 4,000 yagura in Kamakura.

Most noted among them are those on the hill behind Kakuon-ji, which is popularly called 108 Yagura. (There are 177 in fact.) Behind Zuisen-ji there are 79, and 56 are located near Jomyo-ji. Behind Jufuku-ji, yagura of **Hojo Masako** and **Minamoto Sanetomo** can be found in the graveyard.

Tombs of Hojo Masako

Minamoto Sanetomo

Eisho-ji 英勝寺

Official name: Toko-zan Eisho-ji
Sect: Jodo-Shu
Inaugurated by Eisho-In-Ni
Built by Gyokuho Sei-In in 1638
Principal icon (Hon-zon): Amida Nyorai
Open 9:00-16:00
Entrance fee: ¥200
15 min. from JR Kamakura Sta. west exit
Address: 1-16-3 Ogi-gayatsu, Kamakura City, Kanagawa Pref. Tel: 0467-22-3534

 Eisho-ji is the only nunnery in Kamakura, but until recently was closed to the public. It is very well known for its beautiful flower garden. The founder, **Eisho-In-Ni**, was born a daughter of the 6th generation of the **Ota Dokan** family, the founder of Edo Castle (before Tokugawa Ieyasu settled its capital in Edo). Eisho-In-Ni served **Tokugawa Ieyasu** (the 1st Shogun of Tokugawa Reign) who highly trusted her. Whenever Ieyasu would bring her with him into battle, he always won, so he gave her a new name "O-katsu no Tsubone" (Lady Victory) in praise of her miraculous power.
 Ieyasu loved her wisdom. One day, Ieyasu gave a question to his men.
 "What is the most tasty food of all?"
 They seemed unable to answer. But, O-katsu no Tsubone quickly answered.
 "That's salt, my Lord."

Then, Ieyasu asked one more question.

"What food tastes the worst?"

O-katsu answered. "It is also salt." The taste of food depends on how much salt one puts on it. Not only the men present there but also Ieyasu admired her wise answer.

O-katsu became a nun after Ieyasu's death. It was the 3rd Shogun, **Tokugawa Iemitsu**, who granted her the property of Ota Dokan to build her nunnery. The tight relationship with the Tokugawa family guaranteed the temple's high status.

Although the Great Earthquake of 1923 destroyed some of the buildings, highly evaluated architectural pieces of the early Edo period, such as Hojuden or Butsuden (altar house), bell tower and Karamon gate have been preserved in perfect condition.

Hojuden looks like a two-storied building because of its double-roofed architecture, but in reality is single-storied. The lower roof is called "Mokoshi" and gives the effect of a well balanced structure. Below the eaves of the roof are struts carved with Eto (12 animals of the Chinese zodiac), three animals on each of the four sides.

In Hojuden, the principal icon, Amida Nyorai, is flanked by two attendants. These statues were donated by Tokugawa Iemitsu.

On the ceiling, a beautiful scene of the Buddhist Heavenly World is painted in various colors; dragon in the center, celestial maidens enjoying playing music on the flowers, and a flying phoenix.

The Karamon gate, situated on the right hand side of the Hojuden, was built in 1643 but is now covered entirely for protection. Peering through windows, visitors can see its highly technical beam decoration of openworked peony flowers.

The bell tower next to the Somon (main gate) has a peculiar structure. The tower's lower part widens like traditional Japanese skirt-pants called "Hakama Goshi". The bell was cast in 1643, according to the inscription written on it by **Hayashi Razan (1583-1657)**, a respected scholar of Confucian studies of the Edo period.

Deep in the site on the left hand side, beside a cave in which a shrine "Konpira-gu" is situated, we can see a tiny Shinto shrine called "San-rei-sha Gongen".

Behind the temple, below Genji-yama mountain, the beautiful bamboo forest is a favorite spot for photographers.

Kaizo-ji 海蔵寺

Official name: Senkoku-zan Kaizo-ji
Sect: Rinzai-Shu Kencho-ji sect
Inaugurated by Shinsho Kugai
Built by Uesugi Ujisada in 1394
Principal icon (Hon-zon): Yakushi Nyorai
Open 9:30-16:00
Entrance fee: ¥100
20 min. from JR Kamakura Sta. west exit
Address: 4-18-8 Ogi-gayatsu, Kamakura City, Kanagawa Pref. Tel: 0467-22-3175

In the deep end of Ogi-gayatsu residential area, a tiny gate receives visitors with its lespedeza (bush clover) bordered stairway. The small temple site has only its main temple (Hon-den) connected to the monks living quarter, Yakushi-do (altar house) and the bell tower. Yakushido was brought from Jochi-ji in 1776. The wooden statue of Yakushi Nyorai sits on the lotus-flower pedestal with two attendant statues on either side. On the right side is Nikko Bosatsu (Bosatsu of sunlight) and on the left, Gakko Bosatsu (Bosatsu of moonlight).

The Yakushi Nyorai posed in the Yakushi-do is also called "Naki-Yakushi" or "Komori-Yakushi", after a legend of a crying baby. The story is as follows. The priest, **Shinsho-Kugai**, heard a child crying in the temple's graveyard every night. One night, he looked for the baby and he found an old tomb glowing golden and giving off a sweet fragrance. The child's cry seemed to be coming from under the tomb. When he covered the tomb with his cape and began to chant a sutra, the child stopped crying. Next day, he dug the ground to look for the crying boy, but he found a mask of Yakushi Nyorai instead. He thought it was the incarnation of Nyorai, so he brought it back to the temple and put it in the body of the Yakushi statue. Ever since then, it has been kept in the Yakushi Nyorai icon. The mask in the bossom of the statue is exhibited to the public every 61 years.

Yakushi Nyorai

The temple itself was built by Uesugi Ujisada,

Vice Governor of Kamakura during part of the Muromachi era (1336-1573). The inaugurating priest, Shinsho-Kugai, is said to be a fifth generation descendant of Priest **Rankei Doryu**, who was the first chief priest of Kencho-ji.

The Hondo "Ryugoden" was constructed in 1925, two years after the Great Earthquake of 1923, which had destroyed the old Hondo. However, the woodcarvings of a dragon on the transom were made in 1812 and are still in their original form. Fusuma-e (paintings on the sliding doors) were drawn by one of the famous Kano school painters, who were active during the Edo period (1603-1868) as official painters for the Shoguns, warlords and emperors.

16 wells "Juroku-no-i"

The living quarters have a thatched roof and were made in the Edo era, and the beautiful garden in the back has a pond called "Shinji-Ike". Deep in the left hand side of the grounds, there is a cave containing 16 wells "Juroku-no-i". It is said that each well represents a Bosatsu and its sacred water was dedicated to those Bosatsu. On the back wall, a stone statue of Kan-non Bosatsu is enshrined together with a small statue of **Master Kukai**, who is otherwise called **Kobo Daishi**, the founder of Shingon-shu denomination. Before becoming a Zen temple, back in the early 13th century, the temple was built according to the Shingon style.

Kaizo-ji is also known as one of the best temples for flowers. Visitors can enjoy spirea, begonia, azalea, globeflower, iris, aster, Japanese maple, narcissus, gentian, Indian lilac, great trumpet flowers and bush clover etc.. This is also a favorite place of Kamakura connoisseurs.

Iwafune Jizo is not located in the temple's grounds but stands about 500 meters southeast of the temple at the junction of three streets near the JR railway tracks. This Jizo Hall is, however, under the care of Kaizo-ji and ranks 15th on the list of the Twenty-Four Kamakura Jizo Pilgrimage.

In this hall, a wooden statue of Jizo is enshrined as a guardian deity for the first daughter of Minamoto Yoritomo. The existing statue was carved in 1691, but the original one may have been made in the early Kamakura period in view of the story

Iwafune Jizo

related to this hall.

Sokonuke-no-i <10 Famous Wells of Kamakura>

In front of the main gate, we can find Sokonuke-no-i. Legend says that in the days of yore, a nun tried to draw water from the well with a bucket, in the presence of the chief priest. As she drew up the bucket, the bottom fell out and she was drenched to the skin. She remained calm and composed a tanka (32-syllable) verse describing the scene on the spot. Thus the well was named "Bottomless."

Jokomyo-ji　浄光明寺

Official name: Sengoku-zan Jokomyo-ji
Sect: Shingon-Shu Sen-nyu-ji sect
Inaugurated by Shin-A (Shinsho-kokushi)
Built by Hojo Nagatoki in 1251
Principal icon (Hon-zon): Amida San-zon
Open 10:00-12:00, 13:00-16:00 except for Thursday, Saturday, Sunday, holidays, month of August and rainy days.
Treasure House: ¥200
15 min. from JR Kamakura Sta. west exit
Address: 2-12-1 Ogi-gayatsu, Kamakura City, Kanagawa Pref. Tel: 0467-22-1359

　　　　　The origin of this temple was a small place of worship built toward the end of the 12th century by the master **Mongaku** in response to **Minamoto Yoritomo**'s request. Half a century later, the 6th Shogun, **Hojo Nagatoki**, constructed the temple and named it Jokomyo-ji. Eighty years later, in 1333, four Buddhist institutes of four different denominations, Shingon-Shu, Tendai-shu, Zen-shu and Jodo-shu, opened the Buddhism Academy here.

　The main icon (Hon-zon), Amida Sanzon, is actually three wooden statues of Amida (the center of the universe), that were made around 1299, and are the most representative art works of the period.

　The statue in the middle called Amida Nyorai, the largest at a height of 1.49m, is made of cypress wood. We can see the strong influence of the Song Dynasty style of sculpture in the style of the clothing patterns, up-lifted hair and very long nails. From the fact that only its crown is bronze instead of wood, it is assumed that it was fixed on at a later date.

The Amida on the left hand side is called Seiji Bosatu and the one on the right hand side, Kanze-on Bosatu. These two Amida are slightly glancing toward the Amida in the middle as if they were listening to him. Their eyes are made of black crystals and their hands show nine different classified qualities (Ku-hon) in the heavenly world. Amida Nyorai in the middle holds his hands open symmetrically with fingers forming two circles. This hand position (Jo-bon) is quite rare in Amida icons in general.

The patterns on the clothing are not carved but are stuck on in thin clay pieces. These patterns are called "Domon" which is a very typical technique of the Kamakura region in this period. The lotus blossom the Amida sits on is said to be the origin of Kamakura-bori carving tecnique.

They are kept in the treasure house on the left hand side where one also can see a statue of Yahiroi Jizo. In Kamakura in general, Jizo statues are sitting, but this Jizo is standing and has a fleshy body. Yahiroi means "picking up an arrow".

When **Ashikaga Naoyoshi**, the younger brother of **Ashikaga Takauji**, the 1st Shogun of Muromachi Reign, ran out of arrows in a battlefield, a little boy monk showed up and gave him some extra arrows he had collected elsewhere. He stared at the little boy closely as it seemed strange to find a boy-monk in a battlefield. The boy then transformed into the Jizo Bosatu. Naoyoshi later worshipped the Jizo Bosatu as his tuteraly deity.

The treasure house is closed on rainy days in order to protect the statues from humidity.

Izumi-no-i <10 Famous Wells of Kamakura>

Going out of Jokomyo-ji, walk to the left for a while, and follow a narrow path with houses on the left and woods on the right. Beside the entrance of one of the houses, we can find this well. This path goes to Tsurugaoka Hachiman-gu shrine. "Izumi" means a fountain, and this area is called Izumi-gayatsu (Valley of fountain) after this well.

Yakuo-ji 薬王寺

Official name: Daijo-zan Yakuo-ji
Sect: Nichiren-Shu
Built in 1293
Opened by Nichizo
Principal icon (Hon-zon): Kuon-Honshi Shakamuni-Butsu
15 min. from JR Kamakura Sta. west exit
Address: 3-5-1 Ogi-gayatsu, Kamakura City, Kanagawa Pref. Tel: 0467-22-3749

Shaka-do

Melting statue

This was originally a temple of the Shingon-shu denomination and was named Bairei-zan Yako-ji. However, in the year 1293, when the monk **Nichizo** of Nichiren-shu stayed here, after discussing religious principles with the temple's master, he managed to convert him to Nichiren-shu from Shingon-shu. Thus, Nichizo took over the temple.

During the Tokugawa Shogunate, the temple had a close relationship with the Tokugawa family and enjoyed its highly ranked position for almost 250 years. However, after the Meiji restoration, because of the Buddhist Temple Abolition Policy, the temple became masterless and fell out of use for half a century.

In 1914, the temple's 50th master, **Nisshin**, started to rebuild the temple, and his successor, **Nissho**, completed the task.

In the center of the Hon-do, a wooden statue of the master Nichiren is displayed wearing a real monk's robes. This was made in 1834, by the order of **Tokugawa Ienari** (the 11th Shogun of the Tokugawa Shogunate). The statue of Nichiren has his mouth open, as if he were actually preaching. His outfit renewal ceremony is held twice a year, on June 1 and October 1..

There is a Yagura cave behind the Shaka-do where several stone statues are worshipped. However, they all are eroded and half shapeless. It is assumed that the grounds over here were formed by un upheaval of the sea bottom which contains salt that erodes any kind of geological materials.

Ogi-no-I <10 Famous Wells of Kamakura>

This well is inside the ground of a private property which is in the street between the one to Jokomyo-ji and the one to Yakuo-ji. The well has the shape of an opened fan, or "ogi".

Zeniarai Benten Ugafuku Jinja 銭洗弁天宇賀福神社

Official name: Zeniarai Benzaiten Ugafuku Jinja
Enshrined God: Folkloric deity of Uga-jin, or Uga-no-kami
Founded circa 1185
Distinctive property: Family safety, success in business
Annual festival: 1st Horse day of April, Serpant day of September
Sub shrines: Shichifuku Jinja, Mizu Jinja
25 min. from JR Kamakura Sta. west exit
Address: 25-16, Sasuke 2-chome, Kamakura, Kanagawa Pref. Tel: 0467-25-1081

This is one of the most popular spots in Kamakura. People come here because it's believed that if you purify your money in the spring water of the shrine, it magically multiplies in quantity. Every weekend, many visitors, young and old, dip their bills and coins in the spring water. Why do they believe this promise of easy wealth? Here is the legend behind it.

One night in the aftermath of a battle, **Minamoto Yoritomo** dreamed of an old man saying, "I am the god, Ugajin. There is a spring hidden in the wilderness in the northwest of Kamakura. Worship Gods and Buddha with the spring's sacred water. If you do so, your people will naturally have faith in god and the world will be pacified."

Yoritomo immediately took action to find the spring and found it at the site where he enshrined the god Ugajin as he was told in the dream. Farmers washed rice seeds in this spring water and prayed for a good harvest.

Later, Ugajin began to be worshiped as the God of Wealth, and was assimilated with Benzaiten, the Goddess of Fortune. The Shrine, therefore, demonstrates a syncretism in Japanese religions combining a Shinto god with a Buddhist deity

Mizu Jinja

Coin-Washing

through the common element of water.

The tori-i gates and the incense burner indicate a reconciliation of Shinto and Buddhist elements.

The object of worship enshrined here is a stone statue of a serpent with a human head. The serpent is supposed to be sacred to Benzaiten but it is not accessable to visitors as it is enshrined deep inside a cave. It, too, may hopefully make worshipers a little bit richer.

It was not until 1257 that the unique coin-washing practice started. Hojo Tokiyori, then the 5th shogun, visited the Shrine one day and washed his coins with spring water, saying that coins washed here might be doubled. Hearing this, people began to wash their coins, and the coin-washing practice has since been honored by many people in the superstitious hope that they would get rich. Today, people visit here almost uninterruptedly making it one of the busiest shrines in Kamakura. By the way, "Zeni" means coins and "arai" washing

The Shrine's grounds are surrounded with rocks, and there is a cave in the rear where water is pooled. The water comes from the spring deep inside the cave, which is counted as one of the Five Noted Wells in Kamakura. The cave is lit with numerous candles, and bamboo baskets and ladles are available for the washing process. Most visitors wash paper money, not coins, in the hope that the larger the amount washed, the greater the increase. Benten Matsuri festival is celebrated annually on the first Serpent Day of February.

Sasuke Inari Jinja 佐助稲荷神社

Official Name: Sasuke Inari Jinja
Founded: circa 1195
Enshrined god: Mythological god of Uka-no-Mitama, Onamuchi-no-Mikoto, Saruta-no-Hikono-no-Mikoto, Omiyahime-no-Mikoto, Kotoshironushi-no-Mikoto
Distinctive property: Business prosperity, quick recovery from illness, academic achievements, good social relations
Annual festival: 1st Horse Day of February

15 min. from JR Kamakura Sta. west exit
Address: 2-22-10 Sasuke, Kamakura City, Kanagawa Pref. Tel: 0467-22-4711

Sasuke Inari has been worshipped as a god of harvest since old times. The shrine's records say that **Minamoto Yoritomo** fell sick one day while exiled in Izu Peninsula. An old man appeared in his dream and said "I am the god of Inari, and dwell in a hidden place in Kamakura." He told him to raise an army against the Taira family, which Yoritomo did, eventually defeating the Taira family. Yoritomo looked for the old man's "hidden place" and found a tiny grotto. He remodeled it as a shrine and dedicated it to the God of Inari, naming it Sasuke. "Sa" of Sasuke means to help, and "Suke" means Yoritomo himself. Another theory is that there were three important men living in this area, Chibano-suke, Miurano-suke and Kazusano-suke. Three is "san" in Japanese, so three "suke" were together called "San suke". The "n" was dropped eventually and the name became "Sasuke". After Yoritomo died in 1199, the shrine lost its patronage and declined in status. It was the Priest **Ryochu Nen-a**, the founder of Komyo-ji, who restored the Shrine in the 13th century. Later, in 1418, the shrine was integrated by Tsurugaoka Hachiman-gu Shrine as its sub-shrine until 1909 when Sasuke Inari became independent.

Inari Belief

Inari Shrines are dedicated to Inari, the kami (god) of the rice harvest. They can be recognized by the statues of foxes, who are considered the messengers of Inari, on the shrine grounds.

The main object of worship in an Inari shrine is a Shinto deity called Uka no Mitama, a mythological god which is believed to be the patron deity of agriculture, rice in particular. "Inari" in Chinese characters means "rice cargo," and it is one of the most popular deities in Japan, with 32,000 shrines located nationwide. The first and oldest Inari shrine, located in Kyoto, is Fushimi Inari Shrine. It was built in the early 8th century and is the headquarters of all Inari shrines in Japan.

Inari fox

According to legend, one day in February in the year 711, a rich nobleman saw a god appear on a mountain near the present Fushimi Inari. He reported the strange encounter to the emperor, and on the emperor's order, he built a small shrine and dedicated it to the god he had seen. Consequently, because the farmers in Kyoto province enjoyed bumper crops every year after that, they built Inari shrines in their local districts. The imperial court also patronized Inari, and even merchants in urban areas adopted it as their patron deity, crediting Inari for their business prosperity.

Inari shrines are closely associated with the fox, which is believed to be the messenger of the Inari deity. There is always a pair of fox statues sitting in front of Inari shrines, just like the pair of Komainu dogs at other Shinto shrines.

Precisely why the fox is employed is not known, but one folklorist points out that Inari was once syncretized with Dakini-ten, an attendant for Daikoku-ten (the divine protector of Five Grains) of Buddhism. That the object of worship for Dakini was a white fox probably influenced the choice of the fox as Inari's messenger.

Worshippers offer abura-age (fried soybean curd) to Inari shrines because it is believed to be foxes' favorite food. Other symbols of Inari shrines are their deep vermillion painted buildings and long rows of votive tori-i gates leading up to the shrine. The shrine at Sasuke has as many as 40 tori-i gates, mostly donated by devout worshippers, which stretch nearly 100 meters up the approach. The famous Fushimi Inari in Kyoto has more than 10,000 red tori-i gates lining the path to the oratory.

Kuzuharaoka Jinja　葛原岡神社

Official name: Kuzuharaoka Jinja
Founded by Emperor Meiji in 1887
Enshrined god: Spirit of Hino Toshimoto
Distinctive property: Academic achievements, prevention of automobile accidents
Annual festival: June 3
Sub shrine: Ebisu Daikokuten-sha
30 min. from JR Kamakura Sta. west exit Address: 5-9-1 Kajiwara, Kamakura City, Kanagawa Pref. Tel: 0467-45-9002

Around 1320, **Emperor Godaigo** in Kyoto was trying to gain back his political power by overthrowing the Kamakura government. Together with one of his loyal vassals, **Hino Toshimoto**, he secretly took action. However, their plot was revealed by the Kamakura Shogunate and in 1324 he was captured and sent to Kamakura to be tried.

Fortunately, the court acquitted him and he was pardoned and allowed to return to Kyoto. His second attempt to overthrow the bakufu had the support of Enryaku-ji Temple (the headquarters of Tendai sect Buddhism) in Kyoto, of

Tomb of Hino Toshimoto

which the chief priest was his son, **Prince Morinaga**. Enryaku-ji's priests were like an army, called "So-hei" (warrior-priests), comparable to samurai. However, their conspiracy was revealed by a traitor, and Emperor Godaigo was exiled to Oki island, 80 kilometers off the coast of Shimane Prefecture. Hino Toshimoto was sentenced to death. The execution took place on June 3, 1332 at the present site of Kuzuharaoka Shrine.

The architectural style of the shrine is called Shinmei-zukuri, basically the same style as Ise Shrine, the principal shrine of the Imperial Family.

It was only after the Meiji Imperial Restoration of 1868 that Hino's loyal spirit was officially praised. **Emperor Meiji** erected Kuzuharaoka Shrine in 1888, and also Kamakura-gu Shrine in memory of **Prince Morinaga**. This was a significant step in terms of the re-connection of imperialism and Shintoism in Japan's modern history, modernization accompanied by retrospective imperialism.

About 100 meters south of the shrine on the west side of the road is the Hokyo-Into tomb. It is 113.2 centimeters high and was erected in the mid-14th century shortly after Hino's death. The tomb is an historic spot designated by the National Government, and is under the care of the Imperial Household Agency.

The way to this shrine is a beautiful trekking course with thousands of cherry trees which bloom in early April.

(5) South-East Area

<Omachi and Zaimokuza>

MODEL COURSE	
JR Kamakura Sta. ↓5min. Enmei-ji ↓2min Kyo-on-ji ↓3min. Betsugan-ji ↓3min. Anyo-in ↓1min. Jogyo-ji ↓5min. Daiho-ji ↓5min. Ankokuron-ji ↓3min. Myoho-ji ↓5min. Chosho-ji ↓20min. Hossho-ji ↓30min. Motohachiman Shrine ↓1min. Honko-ji	↓3min. Keiun-ji ↓2min. Kofuku-ji ↓1min. Myocho-ji ↓3min. Raiko-ji ↓1min. Gosho Jinja ↓1min. Jisso-ji ↓2min. Kuhon-ji ↓3min. Fudaraku-ji ↓5min. Komyo-ji ↓0min. Senju-in ↓1min. Renjo-in (all by walking)

Enmei-ji 延命寺

Official name: Kimyo-zan Enmei-ji
Sect: Jodo-Shu
Inaugurated by Senrenja Shoyo Noko
Principal icon: Amida Nyorai
Always open reservation necessary to see inside.
5 min. from JR Kamakura Sta. east exit
Address: 1-1-3 Zaimokuza, Kamakura City, Kanagawa Pref. Tel: 0467-22-5464

Korizuka

It is said that this Jodo-shu temple was built by the wife of **Hojo Tokiyori**, the 3rd shogun of the Kamakura reign. The Kamakura Shogun in early times was officially a Jodo-shu believer. In typical Jodo-shu style, it has the Amida Nyorai as the principal icon, as well as the Kan-non Bosatsu. The temple's main treasure, the Jizo Bosatsu statue, is supposed to be the work of the greatest Buddhist sculptor of the period, **Unkei**. Tokiyori's wife strongly believed in Jizo Bosatsu as her protecting God. This Jizo Bosatsu has a woman's features, but in this temple, they have dressed her in a monk's kimono. To see the interior of the Hon-do, including all these figures, advance reservations are necessary.

In the cemetery of the temple, there is a stone memorial monument called "Kori-zuka". Kori means an old racoon dog, "Tanuki" in Japanese. Toward the end of the Edo era, an intelligent racoon dog lived in this temple and the monks took good care of it. In Japan, people used to believe that Tanuki had magic powers and could change freely into other shapes to deceive people. The Tanuki in Enmei-ji didn't deceive people, but it sometimes helped the monks by running errands such as getting a fresh supple of sake. When it died, the mourning monks and neighbours built a monument in honor of their "Old Tanuki".

Kyo-on-ji 教恩寺

Official name: Chuza-san Daisho-in Kyo-on-ji
Sect: Ji-Shu
Inaugurated by Chia
Built by Hojo Ujiyasu in 1678

Principal icon: Amida Nyorai Sanzon
Open 10:00-15:00
Entrance fee: voluntary donation
7 min. from JR Kamakura Sta. east exit
Address: 1-4-29 Omachi, Kamakura City, Kanagawa Pref. Tel: 0467-22-4457

16 Rakans on the beam

From Enmei-ji gate, before the railway crossing on the right, turn to the left at the corner of a meat shop, and you will find this rather humble Ji-shu temple. Originally, there was a temple called "Zensho-ji" here which was later closed. Then in 1678, a temple called "Kyo-on-ji" moved here from Jodo-shu temple Komyo-ji's territory.

The 16 Rakans (Buddha's top disciples) sculpture on the beam of the gate is one of the points of pride of the temple. The principal icon, Amida Nyorai, is said to be the work of Unkei, the greatest Buddhist sculptor of the early Kamakura era. It was given to **Taira Shigehira**, the son of **Taira Kiyomori**, the former Heike shogun. **Minamoto Yoritomo** defeated Kiyomori in 1184 and was preparing to establish his reign here in Kamakura. He captured and brought Shigehira to Kamakura to stay with the Amida Nyorai statue to mourn his lost family.

In 1937, a large collection of coins from China, then Song and Ming dynasties, was found in an excavation on the temple. The discovery was very useful for the study of the monetary system of the period, showing that Chinese currency was used in Japan as a substitute currency.

Betsugan-ji　別願寺

Official name: Toka-san Chosei-in Betsugan-ji
Sect: Ji-Shu
Built by Kaku-a Konin in 1282
Principal icon: Amida Nyorai
12 min. from JR Kamakura Sta. east exit
Address: 1-11-4 Omachi, Kamakura City, Kanagawa Pref. Tel: 0467-22-8501

This temple is situated some steps back from the street between Kyo-on-ji

Inside the Hondo

Cenotaph with tori-i gate relief

and An-yo-in. It became the center of the Ji-shu temples in the Kamakura Shogunate and later in the Muromachi period, and during its prime, was the main official temple of Ashikaga representatives in Kamakura. Also, in the Edo era, as Ji-shu is a branch sect of Jodo-shu denomination, **Tokugawa Ieyasu** gave some land to the temple. However, soon after, it began to decline in status.

The principal icons are the statues of the Amida trinity, with Amida Nyorai in the center flanked by Kan-non Bosatsu on its left and Seiji Bosatsu on its right. One of the temple's treasures, the Gyoran Kan-non, holds a fisherman's basket with his left hand.

A cenotaph near the entrance was erected in 1439 to mourn **Ashikaga Mochiuji**'s soul. One can notice that a mark of a tori-i gate is engraved on each of the four sides, although a tori-i is a symbol of a Shinto shrine. It shows that Buddhism and Shintoism used to exist together without any problem.

An-yo-in 安養院

Official name: Gion-zan An-yo-in Tashiro-ji
Sect: Jodo-Shu
Inaugurated by Ryoben Sonkan
Built by Hojo Masako in 1225
Principal icon: Amida Nyorai
Open 8:00-16:30 (closed on July 8 & December 29-31)
Entrance fee: ¥100
10 min. from JR Kamakura Sta. east exit
2 min. from Nagoe Yotsukado stop on the bus going to Midorigaoka (No.31) or Zushi Sta. (No.40) from JR Kamakura Sta. east exit   Address: 3-1-22 Omachi, Kamakura City, Kanagawa Pref. Tel: 0467-22-0806

Because this temple is situated directly on the Nagoe Kaido street just before Ankokuron-ji, it is easy to find. Especially in spring and early summer, its famous multi-colored azalea blossoms overflow its

The Buddha's footprints

long fence beside the street.

In 1225, **Hojo Masako**, the wife of **Minamoto Yoritomo**, built Gion-zan Choraku-ji temple for her deceased husband. However, this temple was burnt during the war at the collapse of the Kamakura reign. It was then moved from its former location, Sasame-dani, to the present one to merge with a temple called Zendo-ji, but in 1680, the temple was burnt to the ground again. Later, the Kan-non-do of Tashiro-ji temple, built by **Tashiro Nobutsuna**, a man loyal to Yoritomo, was moved to the present location to become the Hon-do of the new temple, which is the present Gion-zan An-yo-in Tashiro-ji.

In the Hon-do, we find the principal icon Amida Nyorai, Senju Kan-non and the statue of the nun Hojo Masako. Behind the Hon-do, stand two stone towers. The bigger one is supposed to be the tomb of Zendo-ji temple inaugurater **Ryoben Sonkan** and was inscribed in the year 1306, making it the most ancient stone tower in Kamakura. The smaller one was built to mourn Hojo Masako.

Jogyo-ji 上行寺

Official name: Hokyu-zan Daizen-in Jogyo-ji
Sect: Nichiren-Shu
Built by Nichiban in 1313
Principal icon: Sanbo Soshi
12 min. from JR Kamakura Sta. east exit
Address: 2-8-17 Omachi, Kamakura City, Kanagawa Pref. Tel: 0467-22-5381

This popular "local" temple welcomes all visitors, inviting them in for a sip of tea any time. It is located just across the street from An-yo-in, and its old, tile-roofed gate is always open. People worship at this temple looking for cures for diseases such as cancer, and mourning lost children.

The Hondo (main hall) used to be located in Myoho-ji, and in 1886 was moved to its present place. Yakushi-do on the right hand side is the meeting hall for visitors and neighbours where everyone can chat with the monks.

On the right hand side of the Hondo, under the same roof, are Inari-do, where

Yakushi-do 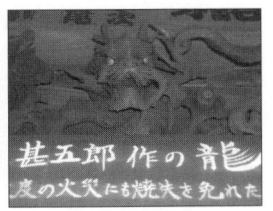 **Jingoro's Dragon**

the god Kasamori Inari is worshipped and Yakushi-do, where Kishi-Mojin is worshipped. The former is believed to cure all kinds of tumorous diseases including cancer, and the latter is for the sake of children's happiness.

On the beam inside the gate, a small, old, wooden dragon sculpture can be found. This is the work of the famous sculptor **Hidari Jingoro** of the Edo era, who made the "Sleeping Cat" in Nikko Toshogu Shrine in Tochigi Pref..

Daiho-ji 大宝寺

Official name: Tafuku-zan Ichijo-in Daiho-ji
Sect: Nichiren-Shu
Inaugurated by Nisshutsu in 1444
Built by Satake Yoshimori
Principal icon: Sanbo Soshi
20 min. from JR Kamakura Sta. east exit
Take a bus going to Midorigaoka (No.31) or Zushi Sta. (No.40) from JR Kamakura Sta. east exit. Get off at Nagoe Yotsukado.
Address: 3-6-22 Omachi, Kamakura City, Kanagawa Pref. Tel: 0467-22-2973

Tafuku Jinja Shrine

This temple was originally called Tafuku-ji and was built in 1399 by **Satake Yoshimori**. The Satake family ancestor, **Shinra Saburo Yoshimitsu**, was the younger brother of **Minamoto Yoshi-ie**, who was the great-great-grand father of **Minamoto Yoritomo**. Yoshimitsu established the Satake clan and settled down in Kamakura in 1083, a century before Yoritomo started the Kamakura reign in 1192.

In Japan, it was quite common for powerful leaders to become monks at their retirement. Satake Yoshimori was no exception, and built Tafukuji for himself beside his residence. Later, the temple was closed for years, but in 1444, **Nisshutsu**, who inaugurated Hongaku-ji, re-opened it with this original name. The small shrine in the garden, called "Tafuku Jinja" (Tafuku means great fortune), was built by Yoshimitsu when he finished the victorious war in 1083 against the Kiyohara clan in north-eastern Japan.

In the Hon-do, the main icon, Sanbo-Soshi, the statues of Nichiren, the inaugurating monk, Nisshutsu, the Satakes' ancestor Shinra Saburo, the god Daikoku-ten and Kishi-Mojin are worshipped.

Kishi-Mojin, who protects children, is worshipped in various places in Japan and is particularly respected in Nichiren-shu sect. At the beginning, Kishi-Mojin was a pair of devils. They had thousands of children, and they used to feed their chidren human flesh everyday. One day, one of child devils disappeared. The mother devil almost turned mad in her desperate search for her child. Who kidnapped the child devil? It was Shaka (Buddha). When the mother devil went to see Shaka to ask why, Shaka explained.

"You always give human flesh to your children, don't you? People who have lost their children suffer a lot just like you do now. I order you to eat pomegranate fruit from now on, because it tastes like human flesh."

The devils mended their ways and became children's tutelary deities. It is also said that a pomegranate is a symbol of rich harvest because it contains lots of seeds inside.

Kiridoshi

Shakado Kiridoshi

After visiting Daiho-ji, if you go for some 15 min. to the left, you'll find the famous Shakado Kiridoshi. A kiridoshi is a pass that was cut through the hills to enable overland travel and transportation of goods to and from the town. There were seven kiridoshi in Kamakura, all of which were constructed in strategically important hills. The cuts are narrow, barely wide enough for one man on horseback to pass through, making them easy to defend from enemy attack.

Ankokuron-ji　安国論寺

Official name: Myo-Hokkekyo-zan Ankokuron-ji　Sect: Nichiren-Shu
Built by Nichiren in 1253
Principal icon: Namu Kuon Jitsujo Honshi Shaka Muni Butsu
Open 9:00-17:00 (closed on Monday)
Entrance fee: Voluntary donation

13 min. from JR Kamakura Stn. east exit
2 min. from Nagoe bus stop. Take a bus going to Midorigaoka (No.31) or Zushi Sta. (No.40) from JR Kamakura Sta. east exit Address: 4-4-18 Omachi, Kamakura City, Kanagawa Pref. Tel: 0467-22-4825

Nichiren, the founder of Nichiren-Shu, moved to Kamakura in 1253 from his home province in Chiba. The first place he settled down in was Matsuba-gayatsu area, where Ankokuron-ji temple is presently situated. He started to write his religious thesis "Rissho Ankokuron" in a grotto and used to chant the "Hokke-kyo" sutra on the hill, while admiring Mt.Fuji far off over the ocean. All these spots are found within the Ankokuron-ji property. The temple's bell tower is also on the top of the hill. The grotto is now covered by a building, and the inside of the grotto can be seen through the window.

Nichiren grotto

Several stone lanterns along the way to the Hon-do were moved here from the Tokugawa family's cemetery in Zojo-ji temple in Shiba, Tokyo. Legend says that Nichiren's cherry walking stick miraculously took root here and grew to become the weeping cherry tree called "Myoho Zakura" found on the temple grounds.

Myoho-ji 妙法寺

Official name: Ryogon-zan Myoho-ji
Sect: Nichiren-Shu
Built by Nichiren in 1253
Principal icon: Itto Ryoson Shishi
Open 9:30-16:30
Entrance fee: 300 yen
15 min. from JR Kamakura Stn. east exit
5 min. from Nagoe Yotsukado bus stop. Take a bus going to Midorigaoka (No.31) or Zushi Sta. (No.40) from JR Kamakura Sta. east exit

Nio-mon gate

The guard "Nio"

The tomb of Prince Morinaga

Address: 4-4-18 Omachi, Kamakura City, Kanagawa Pref. Tel: 0467-22-5813

The narrow street on the left hand side of Ankokuron-ji gate leads to Myoho-ji, which is also a very important temple in Nichiren-shu. The name Myoho comes from Nichiren-shu's sutra "Namu Myoho Renge Kyo" and this temple is the actual place where Nichiren built his humble shack to start his missionary work in Kamakura in the year 1253.

At the beginning, because Nichiren harshly criticised Jodo-shu believers, they attacked and tried to kill him. He narrowly escaped from the attackers, and legend has it that a white ape guided him to safety in a secret cave in the surrounding hills.

Behind the Hon-do, an offering from the Hosokawa clan, there is a scarlet gate with a pair of "Nio" guards, which leads to a steep mountain stairway of 56 stone steps going up to the "Hokke-do" temple house, an offering from the Mito clan. Up there, we can find the bell tower, and for the curious visitor, further climbing leads to the spot where Nichiren built his shack. We can also find the tomb of **Imperial Prince Morinaga**, who was the father of the temple's 5th head priest **Nichiei**, the reconstructor of the temple. From Morinaga's tomb, we can get a nice view of the city of Kamakura. It is amazing that a temple with such a small gate has such a deep, natural interior.

Chosho-ji 長勝寺

Official name: Sekisei-zan Chosho-ji
Sect: Nichiren-Shu
Inaugurated by Nichiren in 1263
Built by Ishii Nagakatsu
Principal icon: Sanbo Soshi
20 min. from JR Kamakura Sta. east exit or take a bus going to Midorigaoka (No.31) or Zushi Sta. (No.40) from

JR Kamakura Sta. east exit, and get off at Chosho-ji stop.
Address: 3-6-22 Omachi, Kamakura City, Kanagawa Pref. Tel: 0467-22-2973

Nichiren & Shiten-no

Hokke Zanmai-do

Chosho-ji was originally the site of a temple called Hongoku-ji, built by a lord of this area, **Ishii Nagakatsu**. After he bacame a Nichiren-shu monk, renamed **Nichijo**, in 1263, he built a tiny shack, which he offered to Nichiren, which later became a temple. However, as Hongoku-ji was moved to Kyoto, Priest **Nissho** built a new temple, Chosho-ji, on the same site.

The main hall is called Taishaku-do. A huge bronze statue of **Nichiren** in the middle of the garden catches visitors' attention. This is the work of **Ko-un Takamura**, a great sculptor in the Meiji era. The inscription on the bronze plate, which says "Denpo Shikoku (Preach and care for the country)" is a quote from **Admiral Heihachiro Togo** of the Japanese Imperial Navy.

Nichiren's statue is surrounded by statues of Shiten-no, Jikoku-ten, Komoku-ten, Zocho-ten and Bishamon-ten.

One building of historical value in Chosho-ji is certainly the Hokke Zanmai-do, built in typical Kamakura style architecture, called "Goken-do". Goken (5 ken, 1ken=6ft.=1.8m) means about 9m. The building has a square form of 9m both in depth and width. In Kamakura, many temples have Goken-do style buildings, a purely Japanese form of architecture.

In this temple also, there is another legend of Nichiren's escape from oppression. In August, 1260, Nichiren was chanting sutra at midnight in his shack. When he felt a little drowsy, three white apes showed up and pulled him by his robe to lead him outside the house. They led him to a big cave in the mountain behind Matsuba-gayatsu. Then, he heard the cry of many people and saw some torches near his hut. Soon after, the hut was on fire, and the people started to shout. He knew what was happening and immediately ran deep inside the cave with the white apes. This incident is called "Setting fire in Matsuba-gayatsu". It is said that the white apes had been sent by the god Taishaku-ten to save him.

Every year on February 2, Nichiren-shu monks who have finished the hard training in Hokke-kyo-ji temple in Chiba, all come to Chosho-ji and bathe with ice cold water. This annual event is called "Kokuto-e" or "Aragyo".

What is Shiten-no?

Shiten-no are the four guardian Gods who are watching the four directions of the Buddhist world. The center of this world is a mountain called "Shumisen". The god who watches the east is "Jikoku-ten", the west "Komoku-ten", the south "Zocho-ten" and the north "Tamon-ten". They wear full armour and have expressions of wrath. Jikoku-ten and Komoku-ten hold swords or halberds, while Komoku-ten holds a writing brush and paper scroll, and Tamon-ten a jeweled spear. They are usually depicted trampling on Jaki (vicious devils) that are often represented as comical and humorous characters.

Choshi-no-i <10 Famous Wells of Kamakura>

This well is near Chosho-ji but not too easy to find. It is in a very narrow passage between two houses on the road side toward the Nagoe Tunnel. This well is othewise called Ishi-no-I, because the well's cover is made of heavy stone (ishi).

Hossho-ji 法性寺

Official name: Enhaku-san Hossho-ji
Sect: Nichiren-Shu
Inaugurated by Nichiro in 1278
Built by Rokei
Principal icon: Nichiren Mandara
10 min. from Nagoe Yotsukado stop. Take a bus bound for Midorigaoka (No.31) or Zushi Sta. (No.40) from JR Kamakura Sta. east exit
Address: 9-1-33, Hisagi, Zushi City, Kanagawa Pref.
Tel: 0468-71-4966

White ape on the gate's beam

This is the most remote temple among Nichiren related temples in the Kamakura area. To be geographically precise, Hossho-ji is in Zushi City.

The temple's gate faces the JR rail crossing, and the two white figures of apes on its beam seem to welcome visitors. The way up to the temple is quite a long steep hill. On August 27 in 1260, Jodo-shu fanatic mobs set fire to Nichiren's shack in Matsuba-gayatsu (now Ankokuron-ji) and were about to kill him. Then, legend tells us a white ape showed up and guided him deep up the valley to an old shrine on the top of the surrounding hills. The shrine was San-no Gongen and the ape was the divine envoy.

Nichiren in fact survived, and later, conditions improved for him. The principal icon is the Mandara of Nichiren (sutra inscription by Nichiren's own hand).

Every September 13 (August 27 in the ancient calendar) and on January 21, at the grotto in Hossho-ji where Nichiren hid himself, a prayer service is held, attended by the head priests of Myohon-ji and Ikegami Honmon-ji in Tokyo.

Nichiren's cave

Nichiren and Kamakura

Nichiren was born in Chiba in 1222. At 12 years of age, he entered Seicho-ji temple in his neighborhood, and at 16, became a monk. When he grew older, he went to Kamakura and then to Kyoto for further study.

In 1252, he returned to his native Chiba. He had started to criticise loudly the other sects, above all the most popular one of the time, Jodo-kyo, and at 30, he was expelled from Seicho-ji. Nichiren later returned to Kamakura and lived in the Nagoe area, which used to be populated by working class people. Nichiren chose this working class environment for his missionary base.

From 1257 to 1260, earthquakes, hurricanes and plagues continuously struck the region, resulting in dreadful scenes of corpses and starving victims in the streets. Through his thesis "Rissho Ankokuron" (Statement of Establishing Right Model and National Security), Nichiren appealed to the government to reject the evil Jodo-kyo and introduce his Hokke-kyo as the official religion in order to reconstruct the nation. The governor, Hojo Tokiyori, showed no interest in that alarming suggestion.

On the contrary, he provoked Jodo-kyo believers to point their confusion and anger against Nichiren personally. Nichiren was often attacked by Jodo-kyo mobs and was finally arrested for "anti-establishment instigation" and was deported to Izu Peninsula for 2 years.

In 1264, after his release, Nichiren went back home to Chiba to restart his mission work, but there too, he was attacked by the men of Lord Tojo Kagenobu, so he returned to Kamakura.

In that year, Hojo Tokimune received a diplomatic letter from the Mongolian Emperor threatening to attack Japan. Previously, Nichiren had predicted in his "Rissho Ankokuron" that there would be a "foreign invasion" and the truth of his prediction increased his popularity among the people. However, Tokimune regarded his increased popularity as dangerous and oppressed him even more harshly, eventually exiling him to Sado Island in 1271. Subsequently, Mongolian invasions took place in 1274 and 1281 in Kyushu (southern Japan) but Japanese forces succeeded in defending their lands. The Kubilai Khan of Yuan Dynasty gave up his ambition of defeating Japan but this momentous experience didn't convince Hojo Tokimune to change his opinion of Nichiren.

Nichiren abandoned Kamakura and went up to Minobu Mountain in Yamanashi to build the temple Minobu-san Kuon-ji in 1274. Eight years later in 1282, he died in Ikegami on the way to Ibaragi. The temple Choei-zan Honmon-ji was built in 1288 in honor of Nichiren in Ikegami (Ota Ward. Tokyo).

Moto-hachiman-jinja　元八幡神社

Official name: Moto-hachiman-jinja or Yui Wakamiya
Enshrined Gods: Iwashimizu Hachiman
Founded by Minamoto Yoriyoshi in 1063
12 min. from JR Kamakura Sta. east exit
Address: 2-1-31 Zaimokuza, Kamakura City, Kanagawa Pref.

This shrine is situated in the end of a narrow street near the railroad crossing in Zaimokuza. It was built by **Minamoto Yoriyoshi**, one of the Minamoto victors after the war in northern Japan. He built a new sub-shrine based on Hachiman-gu shrine in Kyoto. The God Hachiman is the god of victory in war, which had long been enshrined by the leading military clans of the past and revered by the Imperial Family. In 1180, Yoritomo, who set his base in Kamakura, moved this Hachiman Shrine to the present Hachiman-gu site. After that, this Shrine was called "Moto Hachiman", which means "the original Hachiman". However, its real name should be Yui Wakamiya, because in old times, the Yuigahama beach reached this area and the shrine stood near the sea shore. As it was also the tutelary deity of the Minamoto family, thousands of Hachiman Shrines exist, the most famous probably being Tsurugaoka Hachiman-gu in Kamakura.

Honko-ji 本興寺

Official name: Hokke-zan Honko-ji
Sect: Nichiren-Shu
Inaugurated by Tenmoku in 1336
Principal icon: Sanbo Honzon
14 min. from JR Kamakura Sta. east exit
Address: 2-5-32 Omachi, Kamakura City, Kanagawa Pref. Tel: 0467-22-2721

At 33 years of age, Nichiren started to preach in the streets of Kamakura. The corner where the gate to Honko-ji now stands was one of those places. After Nichiren's death, Tenmoku, one of his top nine diciples, inaugurated this temple in 1336, on the very place where he used to give sermons. The statue here of Nichiren is called Dai-Bosatsu (incarnated Bosatsu) and a real Kimono is fitted on the statue.

In summertime, the crepe myrtle tree blossoms in the garden attract many visitors.

Tsuji-no-Yakushido

About one hundred meters from Honko-ji temple, just before the railway crossing, on the right hand side, we can see a small temple. In here, statues of the Yakushi trinity and its Twelve Guardian Ministers are enshrined.

There used to be a temple here called Chozen-ji, before the National Railroad Yokosuka Line was built in 1889. By that time, Japan was heading toward the Sino-Japanese War. To connect Yokosuka Naval port with the capital by railway, the government had to lay tracks on the temple land, forcing the temple to close down. Fortunately, most of the statues were saved because volunteers constructed this Yakushi-do to keep them in.

Keiun-ji 啓運寺

Official name: Shoko-zan Keiun-ji
Sect: Nichiren-Shu
Inaugurated by Keiun Niccho in 1483
Principal icon: Nichiren Mandara
Not Open to the public
1 min. from Suido Michi stop by Kuhonji circular bus line (No.12), bus bound for Zushi Sta. (No.40) or Kaiganbashi circular bus line (No.11) from JR Kamakura Sta. east exit
Address: 3-1-10 Zaimokuza, Kamakura City, Kanagawa Pref. Tel: 0467-22-7453

The founder of Keiun-ji, **Keiun Niccho,** was a well known scholar-monk who wrote a 55 volume work on the Hokke-kyo sutra in 1503. He was originally the head priest of Myoho-ji, and later built Keiun-ji by himself in 1483.

The temple has a statue of Nichiren made in the Edo era, and an Inari shrine for safe navigation for Kamakura fishermen.

The temple's chief priest is traditionally succeeded by the retired chief priest of Chosho-ji. It was once used as a primary school called Soyo Gakko for about 20 years from 1876 for the children of Midarebashi, Zaimokuza and Omachi villages.

Kofuku-ji 向福寺

Official name: Enryo-zan Kofuku-ji
Sect: Ji-Shu
Inaugurated by Ikko Shunjo in 1282
Principal icon: Amida Sanzon
1 min. from Gosho Jinja stop by Kuhon-ji circular bus line (No.12) from JR Kamakura Sta. east exit
Address: 3-15-13 Zaimokuza, Kamakura City, Kanagawa Pref. Tel: 0467-22-9498

Kofuku-ji is a very quiet, tiny temple in Zaimokuza residential area. The founder, **Ikko,** was a monk who traveled around the country promoting belief in the spirit of Amida by chanting-dancing the Nenbutsu sutra, like the Ji-shu founder Ippen.

The main icons are three statues, Amida Nyorai, Seiji Bosatsu and Kanzeon (Kan-non) Bosatsu. The Hondo building was rebuilt in 1826, but was again razed in the Great Earthquake of 1923. The present Hondo was built around 1925. It is not especially attractive to tourists, but has something lacking in the numerous big temples, humbleness and tenderness of popular Buddhism.

Myocho-ji 妙長寺

Official name: Kaicho-zan Myocho-ji
Sect: Nichiren-Shu
Inaugurated and built by Nichijitsu in 1299
Principal icon: Sanbo Soshi
1 min. from Suido-michi stop by Kuhon-ji circular bus line (No.12) or Kaiganbashi circular bus line (No.11) from JR Kamakura Sta. east exit
Address: 2-7-41 Zaimokuza, Kamakura City, Kanagawa Pref. Tel: 0467-22-3572

It is said that the founder, **Nichijitsu**, was the son of a fisherman (or possibly the fisherman himself) who saved Nichiren's life when Nichiren was first exiled in 1261. For years, the Hojo Shogunate had harshly oppressed Nichiren's activities in Kamakura.

One day of May in 1261, Nichiren, who was preaching in the street was suddenly arrested. Without any judicial procedure, they exiled him to Ito in Izu Peninsula, but the escorting officials didn't fulfil their task. On the way to Izu, they left Nichiren on a rock, in the middle of the ocean far from the shore of Ito. Nichiren, left alone on the rock chanted loudly the sutra "Namu Myo Ho Renge Kyo". Then a fisherman called Yasaburo who was fishing nearby heard the chanting voice and saved Nichiren.

Yasaburo's son eventually became a monk and came to Kamakura in 1299. He searched for the place where Nichiren's boat had set off. It turned out to be Numaura beach in Zaimokuza, so he built a temple there.

Due to this origin, the temple has been worshipped by fishermen and fish merchants of this area for centuries. A monument "Uroko Kuyo-to" (Scale Memorial) was built in 1878.

Jisso-ji 実相寺

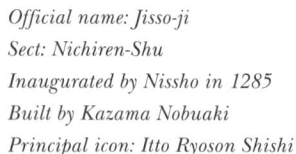

Official name: Jisso-ji
Sect: Nichiren-Shu
Inaugurated by Nissho in 1285
Built by Kazama Nobuaki
Principal icon: Itto Ryoson Shishi
2 min. from Gosho Jinja stop by Kuhon-ji circular bus line (No.12) from JR Kamakura Sta. east exit
Address: 4-3-13 Zaimokuza, Kamakura City, Kanagawa Pref. Tel: 0467-22-7997

This temple originates from a small preaching house, "Hokke-do", which **Nissho** was in charge of during the absence of his master, Nichiren, when he was exiled to Sado Island in 1271. Nissho was ranked top amongst six brilliant disciples of Nichiren. Nissho's mother was the daughter of **Kudo Suketsune**, who fought for Minamoto Yoritomo against the losing Taira forces. He built the preaching house, Hokke-do, on the place where his uncle Suketsune had lived.

Nichiren passed away in 1282, and two years later Nissho converted his Hokke-do to a proper temple, Hokke-ji.

Priest Nissho lived to be 103 years old. On March 26, the anniversary of his death, the Temple holds a mass requiem every year and treats worshippers to red-and-white dumplings.

Raiko-ji (Zaimokuza) 来迎寺

Official name: Zuiga-zan Raiko-ji
Sect: Ji-Shu
Inaugurated by On-a in 1194
Principal icon: Amida Sanzon
Open 9:30-16:30
5 min. from Gosho Jinja stop by Kuhon-ji circular bus line (No.12) from JR Kamakura Sta. east exit
Address: 2-9-10 Zaimokuza, Kamakura City, Kanagawa Pref. Tel: 0467-22-4547

In 1194, two years after the establishment of the Kamakura Shogunate, Minamoto Yoritomo built a Shingon-shu temple called Nozo-ji to mourn his loyal vassal **Miura Yoshiaki**, who bravely fought and was killed in the first war. Miura Yoshiaki was the lord of the region of Miura Peninsula where Kamakura is situated. However, in 1335, the chief priest and the founder **On-a** converted to Ji-shu denomination, so the temple changed accordingly.

Miura clan's tombs

The temple looks like the Miura family's private cemetery, because it has more than 100 stone tower tombs of all the family members and a large, stone, five storied pagoda as a tomb for Miura Yoshiaki himself.

In the Hondo, the principal icon, Amida Nyorai, a wooden sculpture made by Unkei, stands on a beautifully carved lotus blossom. The temple also worships Kan-non, the goddess who cares for children.

In March, the mimoza tree at the entrance flourishes its bright yellow blossoms.

Gosho Jinja　五所神社

Official name: Gosho Jinja
Enshrined Gods: Oyamatsu-no-Mikoto, Amaterasu Omikami, Susano-no-Mikoto, Takeminakata-no-Mikoto, Sutokuin-no-Mitama (Spirit of Sutoku-in)
Founded by merger of five local shrines in 1908
Distinctive property: Family safety, good harvest
Annual festival: 2nd Sunday of June
Sub shrine: Ishi Jinja
1 min. from Gosho Jinja bus stop on the Kuhonji Circular Line (No.12) from JR Kamakura Sta. east exit

The area where the shrine is located was originally divided into two villages; Ranbashi-mura and Zaimokuza-mura, (mura means village). Ranbashi-mura had three shrines; Mishima, Yakumo and Konpira. Zaimokuza-mura had two; Mirume and Yasaka.

In 1873, Mishima shrine was promoted to the main village shrine and later in 1908, the other four shrines joined to become Gosho (Five Places) Jinja. The current main hall was rebuilt in 1931.

The Shrine has three "Mikoshi" (portable shrines). One was made before 1642 and the other two before 1847. At the annual festival, "Mikoshi Watari", held on an early Sunday in June every year, the Mikoshi, carried by parishioners, are paraded down the street to Zaimikuza beach. After a ritual ceremony, the scantily clad carriers take the Mikoshi into the water, make several turns in the waves, and then head back to the shore again.

Mikoshi Watari festival & Mikoshi

Kuhon-ji 九品寺

Official name: Dairi-san Reigaku-in Kuhon-ji
Sect: Jodo-Shu
Inaugurated by Fuko Junsai in 1336
Built by Nitta Yoshisada
Principal icon: Amida Nyorai
Open from the morning till around 18:00
1 min. from Kuhon-ji stop by Kuhon-ji circular bus line (No.12) from JR Kamakura Sta. east exit
Address: 5-13-14 Zaimokuza, Kamakura City, Kanagawa Pref. Tel: 0467-22-3404

The word "Kuhon" signifies the nine different "Hon" which are the qualitative classifications of life periods in Jodo-shu Buddhism. The Hon is divided into upper, middle and lower qualities of passing away, and each Hon is likewise divided into 3 different "Sho", the way of living, so to speak.

The temple was built by **Nitta Yoshisada**, the general who eventually defeated the Hojo family, which ruled the Kamakura shogunate at the time of the final war of 1333.

Yoshisada attacked Kamakura from the Fujisawa side (west of Kamakura) but the rocky coast of Inamuragasaki cape obstructed his troops. Under the full moon of night, he prayed to Amida Nyorai for help, dedicating his sword as an offering by throwing it into the ocean. Then, amazingly the tide began to ebb, thus letting his troops invade the capital by walking on the exposed rocky ledge beside the natural fortress wall of the Inamuragasaki cape.

In the end, Yoshisada won the war against **Hojo Takatoki**, and the Kamakura era ended its 140 year history.

The temple has a stone statue of Yakushi Nyorai which was made in 1296. This is 96.5 cm tall and highly evaluated by experts.

The calligraphy of the temple's name plates hung on the beam at the gate and in the Hondo, are said to be in Yoshisada's own hand. The real name plates are kept safely in the Hondo.

Fudaraku-ji　補陀洛寺

Official name: Nanko-zan Kimyo-in Fudaraku-ji
Sect: Shingon-Shu Daigaku-ji sect
Inaugurated by Mongaku in 1181
Built by Minamoto Yoritomo
Principal icon: Juichimen Kan-non Bosatsu
Open till 17:00
Entrance fee: voluntary
2 min. from Zaimokuza stop by Kuhon-ji circular bus line (No.12), or bus bound for Zushi Sta. (No.40) from JR Kamakura Sta. east exit
Address: 6-7-31 Zaimokuza, Kamakura City, Kanagawa Pref. Tel: 0467-22-8559

This is not a big temple at all but has the prestige of being built by Minamoto Yoritomo 10 years before he established the capital in Kamakura. Because frequent disasters such as typhoons and fires repeatedly destroyed this temple, many documents have been lost and the temple's history is not very well documented.

Apparently it was a big temple in its early days. The temple has a number of treasures, including the statue of Yoritomo supposedly carved by himself, the statue of the monk, **Mongaku**, sitting naked, and the red flag of the Taira Army. This flag was the one that **Taira Munemori**, the chief commander of the Taira Army, kept until their surrender in the final battle against the Minamoto Army in 1185. Munemori offered the flag to Yoritomo as a sign of his obedience. On the flag, it is written "98,000 Divine soldiers".

The name "Fudaraku" originates from a Sanscrit word that means "The mountain where Kan-non Bosatsu lives". More than 100 years ago, the temple was used as a school house. The crepe myrtle tree in the garden is remarkably beautiful.

Zaimokuza History

Wakae-jima

The word "Za", frequently seen in Japanese history and also in place names such as in "Ginza" or "Kabukiza", has various meanings. The first meaning is the officially recognized and protected merchant-craftmen's unions, which existed in Kamakura and Muromachi periods.

The Zaimokuza area in Kamakura was a prosperous port for construction materials, mainly lumber, "zaimoku" in Japanese. Zaimoku used to be transported from Chiba and Izu provinces, and many lumber merchants gathered here and organized a union. The Hojo shogunate constructed on Zaimokuza beach a reclaimed port island called Wakae-jima with rocks transported from Izu peninsula.

It was the first reclaimed land of this kind in Japan. The port continued to function until the end of the Edo era. Today, Wakae-jima at the extreme east end of Zaimokuza beach, just in front of Komyo-ji temple, can only be seen when the tide is low. Now, it is a mecca for windsurfers every weekend.

Komyo-ji 光明寺

Official name: Tensho-zan Renge-in Komyo-ji
Sect: Jodo-Shu
Inaugurated by Nen-na Ryochu (Kishu Zenji) in 1243
Built by Hojo Tsunetoki
Principal icon: Amida Nyorai
Open 7:00-16:00 (in summer time 6:00-17:00)
1 min. from Komyo-ji stop by bus bound for Zushi Sta. (No.40) from JR Kamakura Sta. east exit
Address: 6-17-19 Zaimokuza, Kamakura City, Kanagawa Pref. Tel: 0467-22-0603

This temple is the head temple of Jodo-shu denomination in eastern Japan. It is situated at the extreme eastern side of Zaimokuza beach, and is

Zendo and Benzaiten

the nearest temple to the seashore in Kamakura. After the entrance gate, "So-mon", a huge two storied main gate, "San-mon", welcomes visitors. It was rebuilt in 1847, but the framed name plate "Tensho-zan" hung on the beam is said to have been written by **Emperor Go-Hanazono**, and is inscribed with "Granted on December 15, 1436". On the second floor of this San-mon, several important statues, such as Shaka-Sanzon, Shiten-no, Juroku-Rakan, are kept, but are shown to the public only on special occasions.

The Hondo is free to enter. In the altar, the Amida Sanzon (three Amida Gods, Amida Nyorai in the middle, Seiji Bosatsu on the left, Kanzeon Bosatsu on the right) are exhibited.

Visitors can go around the big tatami matted hall and see the icons closely on the both sides. On the right side, the statues of the Goddess "Wakae-jima Benzaiten" and "Zendo" are enshrined. The former is painted in white, smiling and dressed like a maritime Goddess. The legend says that once upon a time, this Benzaiten Goddess was enshrined in Enoshima Shrine on Enoshima Island, but one day a strong storm washed it away. Later, it was found on the beach near Komyo-ji and has been kept in the temple ever since.

The latter, **Zendo**, is a statue of a Jodo-shu monk in 7th century China, by whom the great Japanese Jodo-shu masters, such as **Honen** and **Shinran**, were deeply influenced.

Another legend explains the reason why these icons are standing side by side: Shortly after the temple was built, a monk used to preach in front of the gate every night. It was the spirit of Zendo, who in fact, had lived six centuries earlier in China. The Goddess of Enoshima Shrine who knew that Zendo was nearby, decided to move close enough to listen to his sermon. She now is called Wakaejima Benzaiten instead of Enoshima Benzaiten.

On the left side of the altar, standing statues of Amida Nyorai and the Jodo-shu founder in Japan, **Honen**, are enshrined.

Hojo Tsunetoki, the 4th Shogun of Kamakura, called in **Nen-na Ryochu** who was the 3rd successor as head of the Jodo-shu denomination, to build this temple. His moving to Kamakura increased the popu-

Senju-kan-non

135

larity of Jodo-shu in eastern Japan.

The next Shogun, **Hojo Tokiyori**, also supported Komyo-ji a great deal, so that the temple grew in size and status, finally becoming the center of Nenbutsu Dojo (Jodo-shu monks training school) in the country. In the Edo era (Tokugawa Shogunate), the 1st shogun **Tokugawa Ieyasu** settled 18 main Jodo-shu training schools in 18 temples in Eastern Japan and Komyo-ji was ranked at the top.

The temple also had a close relationship with the imperial family. In 1495, the temple received the title of "Jodo-shu Principal and Imperial Temple" from the **Emperor Go-Tsuchimikado**.

Honen, Jodo-shu founder

From October 12 to 15, the O-Juya Festival is held. It is a Jodo-shu traditional ritual ceremony which started in Kyoto in the 15th century. All the monks chant Namu Amida Butsu sutra for 10 days and an open-air market in the courtyard attracts a lot of people.

Visitors can go outside directly from the Hondo. To the left, there is a garden, "Kishu Teien", and to the right, a rock garden, "Sanson Goso no Sekitei", (Rock garden of 3 Saints and 5 masters).

The former is famous for its lotus covered pond. The lotus are from 3000 year old seeds that were found in the prehistoric remains on the temple grounds.

The latter is a rock garden that shows the concept of the universe in Jodo-shu Buddhist theosophy. The green part is heaven and the white part is our real world. The biggest rock in the middle of the green part is Amida Nyorai, the center of the universe. The two rocks on both sides of the Amida are the Seiji Bosatsu and Kan-non Bosatsu. They are not human beings. The only human being who is in the heavenly part, the rock on the right side of the green part, is Buddha Gotama, the founder of Buddhism. He was born as a human being but later was elevated above that.

Kishu Garden & lotus in summer time

The rocks on the white pebbled ground are Zendo, Honen, Chinzei and Kishu. The first three are Jodo-shu's greatest masters, and the Kishu is another name for Nen-na Ryochu.

The path behind the rock garden leads to the cemetery of the temple's chief priests since the temple was founded. There are 134 oval shaped tombstones from Ryochu till the last chief priest. After walking some minutes past the cemetery, the founder Hojo Tsunetoki's tomb can be seen.

Although it is closed to the public, to the east of the temple lies the graveyard of the Naito family, Lords of Nobeoka Prefecture (now Miyazaki Prefecture), which was the most important supporter of the temple. The family's wealth can be seen by the oppulence of the 200 tombstones, including some dozens of tower tombstones. The whole of the graveyard can be seen from the street.

"Sanson Goso" rock garden

Naito Cemetery

Senju-in 千手院

Official name: Tensho-zan Senju-in
Sect: Jodo-Shu
Principal icon: Amida Nyorai
3 min. from Komyo-ji stop by bus bound for Zushi Sta.(No.40) from JR Kamakura Sta. east exit
Address: 6-12-8 Zaimokuza, Kamakura City, Kanagawa Pref. Tel: 0467-22-0305

On the right hand side of Komyo-ji, we find Senju-in, a subordinate temple to Komyo-ji.

Neither who built it or when it was built is known because the Great Earthquake of 1923 burned all the historical documents. For a long time, it was a school-like temple called "Senshu-in", where student monks from all over the country practiced the Jodo-shu Buddhist lessons. Komyo-ji was then the supreme Jodo-shu Buddhism college in Japan. However, throughout the Edo era, as the number of students gradually fell, the teacher-monks opened a private school for children. For several decades after the Meiji restoration, when the educational system was still incomplete in the country, Senju-in played an important role as a public school.

Renjo-in 蓮乗院

Official name: Tensho-zan Renjo-in
Sect: Jodo-Shu
Inaugurated by Nen-na Ryochu (Kishu Zenji) in 1243
Built by Hojo Tsunetoki
Principal icon: Amida Nyorai
Open 7:00-16:00 (in summer time 6:00-17:00)
1 min. from Komyo-ji stop by bus bound for Zushi Sta. (No.40) from JR Kamakura Sta. east exit
Address: 6-17-19 Zaimokuza, Kamakura City, Kanagawa Pref. Tel: 0467-22-0603

Situated to the right of Komyo-ji, Renjo-in, previously Shingon-shu, was the residential temple for Komyo-ji monks. The first chief priest, **Nen-na Ryochu**, stayed here for awhile until Komyo-ji's inauguration. Based on this precedent, ever since then, the new chief priest of Komyo-ji first stays in Renjo-in before heading to his new destination in the bigger temple.

Research done by scanning on the principal icon, Amida Nyorai, revealed within the statue the signature of the sculptor **"Harima Hokkyo Soen"** together with the date, October 1, 1299, and a part of the Amida-kyo sutra. It is also believed that the statue was donated by **Chiba Tsunetane**, who was a top strategical adviser to Minamoto Yoritomo. Curiously, the temple has the same crest as the family of Chiba Tsunetane. This also suggests a very close relationship between the two.

The paintings on the Fusuma (Japanese paper doors dividing rooms) and the ceiling are magnificent works of art.

Rokkaku-no-I <10 Famous Wells of kamakura>

From the main gate of Komyo-ji, turn to the left and keep on walking till the tunnel. Take the narrower street on the right, and within a few minutes, on your right hand side, you can see an old hut containing a well. Rokkaku means hexagonal, but the well is octagonal in shape. Legend says that one warrior of the Minamoto clan, **Minamoto Tametomo** shot an arrow from Oshima Island in the Pacific Ocean where he was in exile, targetting Komyo-ji temple. However, it went a little too far and fell into this well. The arrowhead is still kept in a bamboo cane that's hung in the well's wall.

(6) South-West Area

<Hase and Gokuraku-ji>

MODEL COURSE	
Enoden Line Kamakura Sta. ↓5min Hase Sta. ↓7min. Kotoku-in (Great Buddha) ↓6min. Hase-dera ↓2min. Kosoku-ji ↓4min. Amanawa Shinmei-gu Shrine ↓5min. Shugen-ji ↓6min. Goryo Jinja Shrine ↓3min. Joju-in ↓10min. Tsukikage Jizo	↓12min Kumano Shin-gu Shrine ↓3min. Joju-in ↓10min. Gokuraku-ji ↓10min. Tsukikage Jizo ↓12min Kumano Shin-gu Shrine ↓3min Enoden Line Gokuraku-ji Sta. ↓2min. Inamura-Gasaki Sta. ↓20min. Reiko-ji (all by walking)

Kotoku-in (Great Buddha) 高徳院

Official name: Dai-i-san Kotoku-in Seijo-Sen-ji
Sect: Jodo-Shu
Built in 1238
Pricipal icon: Amida Nyorai (Great Buddha)
Open 7:00-18:00 (April-September) 7:00-17:30 (October-March)
Entrance fee: Adult: ¥200 Children: ¥100, Inside Buddha ¥20
7 min. from Hase Sta. on the Enoden Line or 1 min. from Daibutsu bus stop
Address: 4-2-28 Hase, Kamakura City, Kanagawa Pref. Tel: 0467-22-0703

This is the most famous spot in Kamakura, but curiously enough, neither the inaugurator nor the builder are well known. "Daibutsu", the Great Buddha of Kamakura, is 13m high, and weighs 121t. The face is 2.35m long, the eyes are 1m wide, eyebrows are 1.24m wide, the mouth is 82cm wide and the ears are 1.9m long.

The eyes are slightly open. The lips are smiling. The stud-like curled hair consists of 656 pieces. There is neither a wart nor a mole in the middle of the forehead, but a spot from which emanates the Buddha's light which shines on the entire world. It is called Byakugo, and is made of platinum.

The head is made relatively bigger than the body because when we look at the statue from about 5m, it looks well balanced. The face looks down a bit, because when we look up at him, it is the most natural posture. If you look at the surface very carefully, you can tell that it was originally covered by gold (probably painted with a mercury solution). The flat, square face, the lower head top, the round shouldered posture all show the characteristics of Song style artwork in the period.

It is, of course, a National treasure.

In the official Japanese historical chronicle written in the 13th century (Azuma Kagami), it is said that construction of a wooden Great Buddha was started in 1238 and finished in 1243. In the same document, it is also said that in 1252, a Great Buddha of bronze was built, and a certain monk called **Joko** worked hard on the construction.

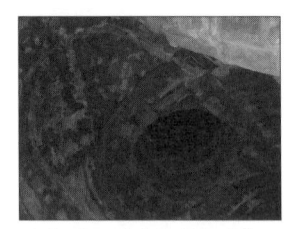

Interior sight of Buddha

The first Great Buddha was built at Todai-ji temple in Nara in 752, when Buddhism was establishing its firm position as the officially recognized religion in Japan. It was the Emperor, himself, who ordered the construction. Buddhism was then the core of the unification needed to control the nation. In order to construct the Great Buddha, the people were forced to contribute in the form of donations or labor.

In contrast, the construction of Kamakura's Great Buddha was motivated by a lady-in-waiting to Minamoto Yoritomo, and people spontaneously donated the funds for the building.

However, in 1247, a typhoon destroyed the wooden Great Buddha, and five years later the present bronze one was built. For the first 250 yeas, it was housed inside a big hall, in spite of a couple of collapses caused by typhoons. However, ever since a huge tsunami in 1498 completely destroyed the hall, the Daibutsu in Kamakura has been sitting in the open air.

According to historical material, the engineers who actually cast the statue were **Ono Goro-wemon** and **Tanji Hisatomo**. They made use of the best technology of the time. The statue is mounted by 1.2m square parts with zig-zag shaped edges. These are thus firmly connected to each other and reinforced by a sort of tinkering technique called "Ikarakuri". Visitors can go into the Buddha's body and see how it is constructed. It is effectively so solid that it even resisted the Great Earthquake of 1923. It is designated as a national treasure not only because of its magnitude, but also its representativeness of Buddhist sculpture in the Kamakura era. The Great Buddha of Nara has been remodeled quite often, but that of Kamakura has kept its original features.

Hase-dera 長谷寺

Official name: Kaiko-zan Jisho-in Hase-dera
Sect: Jodo-Shu
Inaugurated by Tokudo in 736
Built by Fujiwara Fusasaki
Principal icon: Juichimen Kanzeon-Bosatsu (eleven faced Kan-non)
Open 8:00-17:30 (March-September) 8:00-16:30 (October-February)

Main Gate

Amida-do

Entrance fee: ¥300, elementary school children ¥100
5 min. from Hase Sta. on the Enoden Line
Address: 3-11-2 Hase, Kamakura City, Kanagawa Pref.
Tel: 0467-22-6300

Together with the Great Buddha, Hase-dera is one of the most popular places in Kamakura. It was constructed in the 8th century when Buddhism was just starting to prevail in Japan. The date of inauguration is based on the legend that the temple's principal icon drifted ashore at Nagai (now Yokosuka) beach.

In 720, a then famous monk called **Toku-do** had a dream to make a great Kan-non statue. When he was traveling in the countryside of Nara, near Hatsuseyama mountain, he found a huge camphor tree with a marvelous fragrance. He felt certain that this tree was the one that Kan-non wanted him to make a statue with. He thereafter received financial help from **Emperor Gensho** and got two excellent sculptors to work on it. They cut the tree in two parts to make a pair of Kan-non statues. The lower part one was kept in Hase-dera temple in Hatsuse in Nara, and the other Kan-non made of the upper part of the tree was released in the ocean. They prayed that the statue would finally be found by somebody somewhere. 16 years later, the drifting statue was found on the beach of Hatsuse (curiously the same name as its birth place).

They moved it to Kamakura to worship in a temple that was inaugurated by Tokudo. This new temple was the origin of Hasedera.

The principal icon, Kan-non, has ten heads on its own head, eleven all together, is covered in gold foil, is 9.18 m high and stands on a rock holding a staff in its right hand. The staff is metallic and has a ring on the top. This ring has some more, smaller rings that ring when moved. Normally, a Juichimen Kan-non has nothing in its right hand, but this particular style is frequently seen in many other temples throughout Japan also called "Hase". Thus, this is called a "Hase style Juichimen Kan-non". The temple's historical re-

Amida Nyorai

cords say that the icon was made in 721, but it is hard to say whether the present one is the original.

Nevertheless, it is certain that the present statue was made at least before or during the Muromachi era (1338-1573) when big size statue making was the trend.

In Amida-do, there is a statue of Amida Nyorai in sitting position, which is 2.4 m high. It is said that it was made for Minamoto Yoritomo who wanted to exorcise evil spirits at the age of 42 (in Japanese tradition, 42 is an unlucky age). The temple has named this icon "Yakuyoke Amida" (Amida against evils) and it is one of six Amida in Kamakura.

Jizo-do

Jizo-do Hall

Mizuko Jizo

On the middle level of the temple grounds, half-way up the stone stairs, Jizo-do Hall can be found. Outside of the Hall, thousands of tiny Jizo statues, dedicated by those who lost their children, are standing in the yard and on the wall. Jizo-do's roof is sustained by a very specially structured rafter called "Ogi-Daruki". Usually, the rafter is parallel to the roof, but, mainly for aesthetic reasons, this rafter is composed radially.

Jizo

Jizo Bosatsu

Jizo Bosatsu is believed to save those souls that are suffering in each stage of the world. Jizo Bosatsu is also referred to as the guardian deity of children. Babies, including stillborns and fetuses, are also destined to go to the netherworld and have to face the trial.

When they try to wade the River Sanzu, which lies between Shinko-o and Shoko-o, they are too small to cross on their own. They pile up stones by themselves with their little hands but to no avail as devils come out of nowhere and destroy their attempts to save themselves. If their parents have faith in Jizo Bosatsu, however, Jizo will appear before the babies and help them wade across the river safely, guarding them against the devils.

Jizo statues usually carry a staff called Shakujo in their right hand and it is used, says the folklore, for fathoming the river.

Daikoku-do

The god Daikoku of Hase-dera is one of the "Shichifuku-jin" (Seven Gods of Luck) of Kamakura. The Daikoku statue is now displayed in the Treasure Museum which is on the first floor of the Daikoku-do. According to the description on the statue, it was made in 1412, which makes it the oldest Daikoku statue in Kanagawa Prefecture.

Benten in the cave

Benten-do

Beyond the pond, "Hojo-ike", we find Benten-do. Benten is also one of the "Shichifuku-jin", who brings good luck in the professional and business world. In the cave deep inside of Benten-do, we can see a carving in the rocks of Benzai-ten with her guitar, together with 16 other related Gods.

It is said that when Amida Nyorai was drifting in the sea, some oysters stuck to Nyorai's body and led him to Hase beach. Those oyster shells are now worshipped in this Inari Shrine. The Bell of Hase-dera, made in 1264, is the third oldest in Kamakura. It used to toll until some two decades ago, and now is displayed in the Treasure Museum. The new one hanging in the bell tower was made in 1984.

Kakigara Inari Shrine

Kosoku-ji 光則寺

Official name: Gyoji-zan Kosoku-ji
Sect: Nichiren-Shu
Inaugurated by Nichiro in 1274
Built by Yadoya Mitsunori
Open 7:30-sunset
Entrance fee: ¥100
6 min. from Hase Sta. on the Enoden Line
Address: 3-9-7 Hase, Kamakura City, Kanagawa Pref.

Tel: 0467-22-2077

This is one of the temples you should not miss. When visiting Hase-dera and Daibutsu (Great Buddha), with their crowds of tourists, remind yourself that Kosoku-ji is just at the end of a Hase-dera side street.

The inaugurator, **Nichiro**, was one of Nichiren's very important disciple-monks. He suffered alongside his master, Nichiren, throughout the time of oppression and the fear of being executed.

In 1260, Nichiren presented his thesis "Rissho Ankokuron" to **Hojo Tokiyori** through the minister Yadoya Yukitoki's son, **Yadoya Mitsunori**. Later in 1271, Mitsunori was charged with taking custody of Nichiren's top disciple, Nichiro, in his residence, which is the actual site where Kosoku-ji is situated.

Dungeon where Nichiro was imprisoned

While imprisoned, Nichiro received a letter from Nichiren, who was going to be exiled to Sado Island after the suspended execution in Tatsunokuchi. In the letter, Nichiren only seemed to care about his disciple's fate, without any complaints about his own ill-fate. Deeply touched by Nichiren's highly merciful spirit, Mitsunori soon became a Nichiren-shu believer, and converted his house into a temple, which became Kosoku-ji itself.

The actual Hondo was built in 1650. In the courtyard, stands a monument on which a poem "Amenimo Makezu" (Neither Rain) by **Miyazawa Kenji**, the author of the famous "The Night of the Milky Way Railroad", is engraved. He was a devout Nichiren-shu believer.

In the hillside behind the temple, the dungeon where Nichiro was imprisoned is still preserved and in front of it, a monument of his master's letter stands. It says;

"Many chant Hokkekyo sutra only superficially. Very few believe it from the bottom of their heart. Even when they believe from the bottom of their heart, very few do what it says. But, Nichiro, you are the greatest man who truly believed and really practiced what Hokkekyo sutra means. You can bear any hardship. When you are released, come to see me in Sado Island immediately."

From this site, one can enjoy a beautiful view of Yuigahama Beach down below.

Amanawa Shinmei-gu　甘縄神明宮

Official name: Amanawa Shinmei-gu
Enshrined Gods: Amaterasu Omikami Founded by Gyoki and Tokitada Someya in 710
Distinctive property: Good health of the family, stability and peace in the country
Annual festival: September 14
Sub shrines: Gosha Myojin, Akiba-sha
5 min. from Enoden Hase Sta. Address: 1-12-1 Hase, Kamakura City, Kanagawa Pref. Tel: 0467-22-3347

This is the oldest Shrine in Kamakura, dating back to the early 8th century, although its origin is not certain. According to ancient documents entitled "History of Amanawa-ji Shinmei-gu" (ji means a temple and gu is a shrine) kept by the shrine, it was founded by Priest **Gyoki**. He was a famous priest in Nara who helped build various temples across the country, including the well-known Todai-ji in Nara and Sugimoto-dera in Kamakura.

Back in those days, there was a rich, powerful man named **Someya Tokitada** in Kamakura. With the help of Priest Gyoki, he built a temple called Entoku-ji near here, and simultaneously erected a shrine called Shinmei-gu at the top of the hill behind Entoku-ji.

When **Minamoto Yoriyoshi** (985-1078), ancestor of Minamoto Yoritomo (1147-1199, the founder of the Kamakura Shogunate), was sent here to govern, he married a grand-daughter of Someya Tokitada, and prayed to the god of the shrine for the birth of a baby boy. The couple's prayer was answered and **Minamoto Yoshiie** (1039-1106), the future great-great-grandfather of Yoritomo, was born. Since then, the shrine became the tutelary shrine for the Minamoto family.

Minamoto Yoritomo, his wife Masako (1157-1225), their son Sanetomo (1192-1219), and their suite used to worship at Amanawa Shinmei-gu. Later, it was revered by many people, particularly by the locals, as their guardian deity, calling it "Shinmei-sama".

Amanawa Jinja is a miniature version of Ise Jingu Shrine in Mie Prefecture, the mother shrine of the Imperial Family, which was built to worship Amaterasu and serves as the mecca of Shinto. Take a closer look at the roofs. Both the oratory and the sanctum have horn-like cross-boards called Chigi, extending above the roofs at both ends.

Also five poles are placed on top of the roof horizontally, in Katsuogi style. This is a typical Jinja architecture style called Shinmei-Zukuri.

Shugen-ji　収玄寺

Official name: Shijo-san Shugen-ji
Sect: Nichiren-Shu
Inaugurated by Myokei-ni between 1818-1830
Built by Onju-in Nichiyu
Principal icon: Shakamuni Butsu, Mandara of Nichiren
Open until sunset
1 min. from Hase Sta. on the Enoden Line
Address: 2-15-12 Hase, Kamakura City, Kanagawa Pref. Tel: 0467-25-3238

Shijo Kingo Monument

This is a small temple between the houses on the street to Hase-dera from Enoden station. The temple's roof is covered by beautiful green copper. It was built on the land of **Shijo Kingo**'s residence, a samurai during the Kamakura Shogunate, who was a devout follower of Nichiren from the beginning.

When Nichiren was about to be executed at Tatsunokuchi in 1271, Kingo was going to kill himself as a martyr to his master. However, when Nichiren was saved, he became a monk and took the name **Shugen-in Nichirai**. As time passed, the temple fell to ruins until the monk **Nichiyo** of Ankoku-Ron-ji rebuilt it in the years 1818-1830.

The present main hall was constructed in 1923 by the monk Nichiji of Kosoku-ji and its name was changed from Shugen-in to Shugen-ji. After World War II, it became an officially independent temple.

The principal icon, the Mandara of Nichiren, is a manuscript of the Hokkekyo sutra, "Namu Myoho Rengekyo" written by Nichiren.

Goryo Jinja　御霊神社

Official name: Goryo Jinja
Enshrined Gods: Kamakura Gongoro Kagemasa
Founded in 2nd half of the 12th century (Heian Period)
Distinctive property: Quick recovery from eye disease, good luck, academic achievement, good connections, victory in competitions
Annual festival: July 20 and September 18
Sub shrines: Ishigami Jinja, Jijin-sha, Konpira-sha, Akiba Jinja, Sorei-sha
3 min. from Enoden Hase Sta.
Address: 4-9 Sakanoshita, Kamakura, Kanagawa Pref.
Tel: 0467-22-3251

The shrine is dedicated to the soul of an extraordinarily brave samurai with great physical strength, who lived here before the Kamakura era. His name was Kamakura Kagemasa (1069-?), commonly known as "Gongoro", giving the shrine its local name "Gongoro-san".

At the age of 16, he took part in a battle at Yokote, Akita Prefecture, as a retainer of Minamoto Yoshiie (1039-1106), great-great-grandfather of Minamoto Yoritomo. During the bitter battle, his left eye was hit by an enemy's arrow. Undaunted, he bravely continued fighting and knocked the enemy down. When he came back to the camp, the arrow was still stuck in his eye. His colleague tried to help remove it by putting his foot on Kagemasa's forehead, but Kagemasa got angry and accused the colleague of being rude.

Samurai were full of pride and self-respect in those days, and having one's face stepped on was very offensive. Obviously, it was against the samurai code and was unbearable for Kagemasa. The colleague deeply apologized for his rudeness and the arrow was eventually pulled out in a more fitting manner. In addition, Kagemasa's injured eye was cured soon after.

To commemorate this episode, a pair of fletchings (arrow feathers) were employed as the crest of the shrine and they appear on the tiles of the roof and on the money-offering box. Kagemasa's prowess and manner were highly praised as a role model of the Kanto samurai, hence the shrine is credited by the locals with its power of healing eye diseases. In addition, to praise his bravery, a Jizo statue named Yagara (arrow) was created which was enshrined at Engaku-ji, but was unfortunately destroyed by the 1923 earthquake. Today, a stone monument for this statue stands at Keisho-an in Engaku-ji and is listed 14th on the Kamakura Twenty-Four Jizo Pilgrimage. At the Keisho-an's hall, archers often practice archery before the altar.

In the shrine's ground, there are a pair of round stones which are dubbed Tamoto-ishi (sleeve stone) and Tedama-ishi (stone in one's hand). Legend has it that the larger stone, weighing 105 kilograms, was in Kagemasa's sleeve-pocket and the smaller one, weighing 60 kilograms, was in his palm as if they were toys. The stones are displayed to emphasize his physical strength.

There are quite a few Jinja named "Goryo". "Go" is a honorific prefix and "ryo" denotes souls. According to Shinto dogma, those who died an unnatural death, died by violence or in a state of anger or resentment need to be buried with courtesy and reverence, and their souls should be enshrined to appease their curse.

Otherwise, it is believed, people will incur divine wrath and punishment, or revenge will be exacted by the malevolent spirits of the dead. Goryo Jinja were thus erected throughout Japan to exorcise evil spirits, and special services are performed regularly to soothe the revengeful spirits. In the shrine, wooden statues of Kagemasa and his wife are enthroned on the altar, but they are not visible. As usual in Shinto shrines, only a round mirror is placed in the center.

Joju-in 成就院

Official name: Fumyo-zan Horyu-ji Joju-in
Sect: Shingon-Shu Daikaku-ji sect
Inaugurated by Kobo Daishi in 1219 (or 1221)
Built by Hojo Yasutoki
Principal icon: Fudo Myo-o
Open 8:00-17:00
5 min. from Gokuraku-ji Sta. on the Enoden Line
Address: 1-1-5 Gokuraku-ji, Kamakura City, Kanagawa Pref. Tel: 0467-22-3401

Joju-in stands near the top of the hill, Gokurakuzaka Kiridoshi, about half way between Hase and Gokuraku-ji stations. In June, the view from its hydrangea bordered approach, affords a pho-

Koyasu Jizo

Kokuzo Bosatsu

togenic scene with Yuigahama beach in the background.

Hojo Yasutoki, the 3rd shogun of the Kamakura Reign, built this temple on the place where the founder of Shingon-shu, **Kobo Daishi**, stayed for a hundred days to enshrine the Kokuzo Bosatsu (God of wisdom and fortune) three centuries before. It was once burnt down because of the war in 1333 when the Kamakura Reign collapsed, but was rebuilt later in the Edo era.

The principal icon, Fudo Myo-o is the god of marriage, and another god, Koyasu Jizo is the god of fecundity.

The wooden sculpture of "The monk **Mongaku** in Practice" is an extraordinary piece, resembling a work of modern art.

At the foot of the hill, on the other side of the road, there is another temple called Myoko-zan Seisen-ji, otherwise called Kokuzo Bosatsu, which is said to have been built by **Gyoki** in the 7th century. Here we can also find a well, "Seigetsu-no-i" (well of stars and moon), on the roadside.

Seigetsu-no-i <10 Famous Wells of Kamakura>

This well is found in front of Kokuzo-Bosatsu temple on the way to Gokuraku-ji. Now it's dry, but as it is on the road side of Gokuraku-ji Kiridoshi, one can assume that people used to have a rest and a drink here on the way in old times.

Seigetsu means stars and the moon. This used to be a dark area covered by dense vegetation, and even in the day time, the well water reflected the stars and moon. There is a legend that the famous monk Gyoki found a rock in this well and sculptured a statue of Kokuzo-Bosatsu with it.

Gokuraku-ji 極楽寺

Official name: Ryojusen Kanno-in Gokuraku-ji
Sect: Shingon-Ritsu-Shu
Inaugurated by Ninsho in 1259

Built by Hojo Shigetoki
Principal icon: Shaka Nyorai
Open 9:00-16:00
¥300 for Treasure Museum (open only Saturday and Sunday, closed in August)
2 min. from Gokuraku-ji Sta. on the Enoden Line
Address: 3-6-7 Gokuraku-ji, Kamakura City, Kanagawa Pref. Tel: 0467-22-3402

Gokuraku-ji, which means "heavenly temple", has a beautiful thatched roof gate and a very well designed garden. The monk **Ninsho** who opened welfare facilities here, such as a clinic and medication center, was born in 1217 in Nara. At the age of 13, he was already a vegetarian, honoring one of the Five Buddhist Commandments, and studied Shingon Ritsu Buddhism at Saidai-ji. There, he built the country's first Hansen's disease hospital, "Kitayama Juhakkenko".

He used to bring leprosy patients who were begging in the country roads back to his clinic in Nara where he could care for them. He did this work for years from early morning to late at night.

In 1252, he moved to Ibaraki Prefecture to propagate Shingon Ritsu doctrines in the Kanto region. Later, at age 44 in 1261, at the invitation of **Hojo Shigetoki**, he went up to Kamakura, and continued his work for the long-suffering poor. It is said that over 20 years, he cured 46,800 people, although 10,450 died in his facilities. He also constructed bridges, roads, and public baths and gave clothing to the poor.

His most remarkable work was the construction of the road connecting the western part of Kamakura to the central district. Now it is called Gokurakuji-zaka Kiridoshi, a road cut through the cliff, that even now is a boon to traffic and transportation.

The principal icon at Gokuraku-ji, Shaka Nyorai, is modeled after the one at Seiryo-ji in Kyoto. It's shown to the public only on April 7,8,9. A stone bowl for grinding medicinal herbs, and a well (now dried up) used for patients are preserved in the garden.

Medicine Grinding Bowl

Priest Ninsho never stopped his religious

activities as well as civil construction work for nearly four decades. He built 83 temples, 189 bridges and 71 roads. After he died at 87, **Emperor Godaigo** conferred on him the title of Bosatsu in praise of his virtue. People called him Ninsho Bosatsu, a living god, after Gyoki Bosatsu, who lived in the 7th century and who also used the Buddhist faith for the sake of the poor.

However, some, such as Nichiren, criticized him, pointing out that Ninsho was too close to the Hojo regime and was hunting for concessions. There was constant antagonism between the two religious leaders. Ninsho used to say his philosophy was "A Buddhist should be a man of deeds, not a man of words".

After entering through the gate at the end of the cherry-lined path is the main hall, wherein is enshrined a 98-centimeter-tall wooden, seated statue of Fudo-myo-o, made in the late 12th century. It used to be the main object of worship in a temple in Shimane Prefecture, but was brought here in 1926. Fudo-myo-o holds a sword in his right hand and a rope in his left. His teeth are bared and eyes glare angrily, as he stands threatening to destroy any devils who may try to do harm to the Lord Buddha's teaching.

The Fudo-myo-o statue is flanked by a statue of Yakushi Nyorai (to his left) and a 56-centimeter-tall wooden, sedentary statue of Monju Bosatsu, known as the Bosatsu of Wisdom and Intellect, to his right. It is believed to have been carved in the latter half of the 13th century, most probably in 1273, and reflects influence of the Song style sculpture.

In the treasure museum, "Tenborin-den", Buddhist ritual fittings and ancient statues such as statues of Shaka and Nyorai, measuring 91 centimeters tall, are exhibited. This Nyorai's left palm is turned outward in front of his chest. This position is called "Tenborin" style (the hall is named after this). Also displayed are the statues of the following Ten Great Disciples of Shaka; Daikasho, Anaritsu, Furuna, Kasen-nen, Ubari, Ragora, Sharihotsu, Mokukenren, Ananda and Shubodai. They measure 83 to 87 cm tall and some of them were made as early as 1269.

The flowering tree near the Treasure hall is an old Japanese apricot tree or ume, which is unique in that blossoms bear single and double petals on the same stalk. Halfway along the paved approach to the main hall on the right hand side is the Daishi-do sub-temple dedicated to **Kukai**, or Priest **Kobo Daishi** (774-835), the founder of Shingon-shu denomination. A lacquered statue of him is enshrined here. Also enshrined in this Daishi-do is a statue of Nyoirin Kan-non, which ranks 22nd of the Kamakura Thirty-Three Kan-non Pilgrimage. Legend asserts that it used to be owned by **Lady Tokiwa Gozen**, the mother of **Mina-

Daishi-do

moto **Yoshitsune**, as her guardian deity.

About 300 meters north-northwest of the temple, past Inamuragasaki Elementary School, is a clearing where a huge Gorinto (five level stone monument) and Hokyo-into (cenotaph) stand. The Gorinto measures 355 centimeters in height, the tallest of its kind in the Kanto region (Tokyo and its surrounding prefectures) and is also called Ninsho-to since it was built in commemoration of Priest Ninsho. The 310cm tall Hokyo-into is said to be the tomb of Hojo Shigetoki, the founder of the temple. Only Shingon sect Buddhists makes such big stone cenotaphs or tombs.

In addition, those up here are made of andesite, which is far harder than tuff. Since neither andesite nor sculptors of such hard rock were available in Kamakura, the raw rocks are believed to have been brought from the Izu Peninsula and the sculptors from Nara. The area housing these monuments is open to the public only on April 8, Shaka's birthday.

Incidentally, Gokuraku means "paradise" in Japanese, and therefore, Gokuraku-ji Temple can be called the Temple of Paradise.

Legend of Tsukikage Jizo

Within some 15 minutes of walking from Gokuraku-ji temple, deep in the village in Nishi-gayatsu, there is a small hut called Tsukikage Jizo-do. In the hut, a very old Jizo statue stands wearing a big red robe. The hall is always open, but few visit because it is not well known. Along the wall In the yard in front, there are several tiny tombs. One of these tombs is of a girl called Tsuyu, who is the heroine of a sad story that has been handed down since long time in the community.

During the year 1283, a mother and her daughter used to come early in the morning to do kitchen work in the residence of regent Hojo Naritoki in Kamakura, The mother was short-tempered, rude and even a bit naughty, maybe because of hardships she had suffered from for many years. On the contrary, her 10 year old daughter, Tsuyu, was a tenderhearted girl who always used to care for her mother. The people admired her and often talked about them, wondering, "Is she really her daughter?", even though they physically resembled each other.

Tsuyu seemed not to care about such rumors, and kept on working very hard. One day, some trouble happened. A very expensive porcelain dish was found broken beside the well.

"Give yourself up, whoever has done it." Naritoki announced to all his men.

"We can't do anything about the broken dish. What is impermissible is hiding oneself."

All the employees were interrogated and checked. They concluded that Tsuyu's mother was the most suspicious, because she had no alibi and they found a cut on her fingertip. They severely asked her.

"I am really sorry, my Lord." She finally confessed. "It was my fault for covering up for my daughter."

"You say it was Tsuyu who did that?"

"Please forgive my daughter."

"Then, how come your fingertip is cut?"

"Because I hit her when she told me."

Next, they interrogated Tsuyu.

She responded that it was true what her mother had said. Everybody could tell that she was protecting her mother, and Naritoki repeatedly told Tsuyu to tell the truth.

"I know that you are a good girl. So, tell me the truth. To lie is immoral, you know? It wouldn't be for you or your mother's sake."

But Tsuyu never nodded.

"To care for one's mother is a child's duty. You can never make your mother a criminal."

The judgement was severe. Both were fired and the mother was expelled from the region. Naritoki sent Tsuyu to someone's house to be adopted because he felt sorry for her. When they were leaving, Naritoki gave Tsuyu a beautiful, expensive kimono with a plum blossom pattern.

However, she never wore the kimono because her mother took that away from her, and sold it for money. Tsuyu was very nicely received and treated by her step-parents, but she was so disgraced by the parting from her mother that she eventually fell ill and soon after passed away in sadness. Her acquaintances felt deeply sorry for her, and built her a tomb in the valley of Tsukikage near Gokuraku-ji temple. Her tiny tomb was taken care of for hundreds of years in the yard of Jizo Hall.

However, when Tsukikage Jizo was moved to another place, the tomb of Tsuyu disappeared. Nobody knows how and when. "Maybe it's Jizo himself who took her with him." They would say. But at the newly built Jizo Hall in Nishi-gayatsu, another tiny tomb of Tsuyu was miraculously found by a group of historians.

The tomb of Tsuyu covered by moss

This very tomb exists in front of the Tsukikage Jizo Hall, and is always covered with plum blossom patterned moss. They say that Jizo gave the beautiful plum blossom patterned kimono back to an unhappy tender little girl who never had a chance to wear it.

Kumano Shingu 熊野新宮

Official name: Kumano Shingu also called Shingu-sha
Enshrined Gods: Yamato Takeru-no-Mikoto, Hayata-mano-no-Mikoto, Susano-no-Mikoto, Takeminakata-no-Mikoto
Founded in 1269
Distinctive property: Good luck, quick recovery from illness, protection of agriculture and industry
Annual festival: September 9,
3 min. from Enoden Gokuraku-ji Sta.
Address: 2-3-1 Gokuraku-ji, Kamakura City, Kanagawa Pref.

This is the Chinju (community shrine) of Gokuraku-ji area. It was razed in 1298 and rebuilt in 1300. After the collapse of the Kamakura Shogunate, it was protected by the Ashikaga family. In 1335, Ashikaga Naoyoshi donated the land it sits on.

On this site, Yagumo Jinja and Suwa Myojin were originally enshrined. However, both of them were destroyed by the Earthquake of 1923. Later in 1928, those two shrines were mergered with this Kumano Shingu. The present shrine building was constructed in 1927.

Reiko-ji 霊光寺

Official name: Ryuo-zan Reiko-ji
Sect: Nichiren-Shu
Inaugurated in 1957
Principal icon: Nichiren
15 min. from Shichirigahama Sta. on the Enoden Line
Address: 1-14-5 Shichirigahama, Kamakura City, Kanagawa Pref. Tel: 0467-31-6547

Although it was officially founded in 1957, its real beginning goes back to

Statue of Nichiren praying for rain

the end of the Meiji era (around 1900) when a priest found a stone monument at the excavation of some reclaimed land over a pond called "Tanabega-ike". A miracle happened in the year 1271 by this lost pond. A severe drought attacked Kamakura that year and the Kamakura shogun of the time, **Hojo Tokimune**, ordered the priest **Ninjo** of Gokuraku-ji temple, who was famous for his magical powers, to execute a prayer for rain. He prayed for rain for two weeks, but not a single drop of rain fell.

Then, Nichiren showed up here and started to chant a sutra beside the pond. All of a sudden, it started to shower from the thundering sky. It rained for three days. The pond was later reclaimed but the legend survived. The stone monument, which was built in 1735, is now standing in Reiko-ji.

The route to the temple is the one Nichiren followed. The temple is located not far from Shichiriga-hama beach.

South-West

(7) West Area

<Koshigoe and Ofuna>

MODEL COURSE

Enoden Line Koshigoe Sta.
↓ 4min.
Josen-ji
↓ 1min.
Koyurugi Jinja
↓ 2min.
Manpuku-ji
↓ 3min.
Honjo-ji
↓ 3min.
Kangyo-ji
↓ 3min.
Myoten-ji
↓ 1min.
Tozen-ji
↓ 4min.
Honryu-ji
↓ 10min.
Hozen-in
↓ 10min.
Hogen-ji
↓ 5min.
Ryuko-ji
↓ 5min.
Joryu-ji
↓ 5min.
Honren-ji
↓ 15min.
Enoshima Jinja
↓ by Monorail from Enoshima to Nishi-Kamakura, 5min
Ryukomyojin-Sha
↓ 10min.
Shoren-ji
↓ by Monorail from Nishi-Kama-kura to Ofuna, 10min.
Ofuna Kan-non-ji

Josen-ji 浄泉寺

Official name: Koyurugi-san Shogan-in Josen-ji
Sect: Old Shingon-Shu Daikaku-ji sect
Inaugurated by Kukai
Principal icon: Fudo Myo-o
4 min. from Koshigoe Sta. on the Enoden Line
Address: 2-10-7 Koshigoe, Kamakura City, Kanagawa Pref. Tel: 0467-31-5567

Not many tourists visit the temples in Koshigoe, an old fishing community facing the famous island of Enoshima.

Walking from Enoden's Koshigoe station towards the beach, and turning left along Route <134>, we come upon Josen-ji on our left, facing Koyurugi Jinja shrine on our right. It is said that the famous monk **Kukai**, or **Kobo Daishi**, founded this temple, which exemplifies an important point of the religious-political history of Japan.

During the Nara period (8th century), Kukai had linked Amaterasu, the God of Shinto, which is the ancestor of the Imperial family, with Dainichi Nyorai (Great Sun God) of Buddhism, the center of the universe. Shinto and Buddhism thus ideologically coexisted in the context of the Shinbutsu Shugo (God and Buddha unification) concept until the end of the Edo period. However, at the dawn of Japanese nationalism in the Meiji Restoration, toward the end of the 19th century, Shinto was forcefully separated from Buddhism to become Japan's official national religion.

One can say that this "Shinbutsu bunri" (Segregation between Shinto and Buddhism) policy played a crucial part throughout the course of history up to World War II. Japanese people were strictly taught that the Emperor was the most powerful and indisputably divine being, and Japan's army was invincible as well. Meiji modernization ironically led Japan to the legendary Kamikaze spirited imperial militarism that caused so much suffering in neighbouring Asian countries during the war. Disagreements over related historical facts still today cause international problems with China, Korea and other south-eastern Asian countries. The fact that Japan's prime ministers worship at Yasukuni Shrine for war victims is another current tempest based on the past.

Josen-ji shared the Koyurugi grounds with Koyurugi Jinja, and even after the "Shinbutsu bunri" policy, the head priest of the temple continued to administer Koyurugi Jinja Shrine until 1918. This was a very rare case in that period.

The temple priests used to teach the children of the village and the class eventually developed into Koshigoe Elementary School of today.

Koyurugi Jinja　小動神社

Official name: Koyurugi Jinja
Enshrined Gods: Takehaya Susano-no-Mikoto, Takeminakata-no-Kami, Yamato Takeru-no-Mikoto, Toshigami
Built by Sasaki Moritsuna in 1185-1190
Virtue: Protection from disaster, country development, good harvest
Sub-shrines: Kaijin-sha, Inari-sha, Kotohira-sha, Dairokuten-sha
Annual festival: mid July
5 min. from Koshigoe Sta. on the Enoden Line
Address: 2-9-12 Koshigoe, Kamakura City, Kanagawa Pref. Tel: 0467-31-4566

This shrine stands on the cape called Koyurugi-Misaki, next to Koshigoe fishing harbour. The name derives from the legend that there was a beautiful pine tree here that would sway even when no wind was blowing.

Once upon a time, **Sasaki Moritsune (1166-1227)**, a vassal of Minamoto Yoritomo, visited Enoshima Jinja Shrine, and on his way back, he took a look around and was deeply moved by the pine tree's beauty. Deeply impressed, he was motivated to set up a shrine on this site. He invited Hachi-oji-gu Shrine in Omi (Shiga Pref.) which was his family's native land, to build here. The shrine was thus erected circa 1185 with the name "Hachi-oji-gu", enshrining Takehaya-susano-no-mikoto as a tutelary deity of Koshigoe village.

In 1333, when **Nitta Yoshisada** attacked Kamakura, he prayed here for victory (see Kuhon-ji). Nitta overturned the Kamakura regime, marking the end of the Kamakura period . Out of gratitude to the Gods for their help, Nitta, not only donated a sword and a lump of gold to the shrine, but also reconstructed the building.

Later, with the syncretic mixture of Shinto and Buddhism, Shinto deities began to be viewed as temporary manifestations of Buddha, and each Shinto deity was identified with a Buddhist one. In the case of Takehaya-susano-no-mikoto, for example, he was thought to be a vicar of **Gozu-Ten-no**, because of their similarity in divine characteristics.

In the Edo era, the shrine was under the supervision of nearby Josenji, a Shingon-sho temple standing on the opposite side of Route <134>.

After the Meiji Imperial Restoration in 1868, however, all of the temple-shrine complexes had to separate Shinto from Buddhism, and were forced to change their names. Hachioji-gu then changed its name to "Koyurugi Jinja".

The temple's Annual Festival, Ten-no-sai, held on a weekend in mid July, is jointly held with Yasaka Shrine of Enoshima, which also enshrines the same God. Both used to hold a grand festival called "Ten-no-sai" to stave off epidemics in the height of summer when epidemics were most likely to spread. The tradition continued well into the era after the Meiji Imperial Restoration. Gorgeously ornamented portable shrines from Yasaka Jinja on Enoshima cross the sea to the Koshigoe shore. They are received by the Mikoshi of Koyurugi Jinja near Ryuko-ji and parade back to Koyurugi Jinja. The locals start to rehearse the musical accompaniment every night weeks before, in the street. In Koshigoe, summer begins with this festival.

Manpuku-ji 満福寺

Official name: Ryugo-san Io-in Manpuku-ji
Sect: Shingon-Shu Daikaku-ji sect
Inaugurated by Gyoki in 744
Principal icon: Yakushi Sanzon
Open: 9:00-17:00
Entrance fee: voluntary
5 min. from Koshigoe Sta. on the Enoden Line
Address: 2-4-8 Koshigoe, Kamakura City, Kanagawa Pref. Tel: 0467-31-3612

Manpuku-ji is one of the oldest temples in the Kamakura area, having been built in the 8th century. It was **Gyoki**, known as the founder of Sugimoto-dera of Juniso and more importantly the inaugurator of the Great Buddha in Nara, who is said to be the founder of this temple. The temple's historical records state that in 744, when Gyoki stayed here on his way up to Kyoto, at the eager request of fishermen of the village, he inaugurated a temple for the people's health and welfare. By that time he would have been 76 years old and there is no historical evidence that he was traveling around here. In addition, he must have been very busy organizing the financial operation for the Great Buddha's construction, which was finished in 756.

Some say that as Gyoki's family name was "Koshi" in Osaka, there might have been a certain forced connection with "Koshi" of Koshigoe.

Whether the above is true or not, Manpuku-ji does not need Gyoki's help to be famous, because it has another touching story which actually did happen here.

When **Minamoto Yoritomo** defeated the Taira family, he marched into Kamakura in 1185 to settle his government. He soon later heard that his younger brother, **Minamoto Yoshitsune** (by a different mother) had been promoted by the imperial court of Kyoto to a high rank. Yoritomo had received neither any promotion nor any kind of honorable praise by the court, although he was Yoshitsune's elder brother and Minamotos' top commander. Yoritomo, now the most powerful person of the time actually, felt disgraced by the fact that he had not been informed about this at all. He also had confidential information of Yoshitsune's "conspiracy to rebel", from his follower, **Kajiwara Kagetoki**.

Yoshitune was surprised to hear that his brother, for whom he had fought wars against the Taira, was angry. He had no intention of rebelling, and left Kyoto to see Yoritomo in order to explain the situation. He was accompanied by some captured Taira generals, whom he was to hand over to Yoritomo as proof of his loyalty, and in mid-May arrived at Koshigoe, a fishing village just west of Kamakura and stayed at this Manpuku-ji. However, Yoritomo refused to meet with his younger brother.

Waiting impatiently for his brother's permission in this temple, Yoshitsune sent a letter insisting that all his efforts and perseverance of those past years were for nothing more than to realize their deceased father's wish of reconstructing the Minamoto family. Yoritomo opened the letter but never the door, and ordered his men to kill Yoshitune. An anguished Yoshitsune abandoned the capital and began to run from one place to another. Eventually cornered, he was forced to counterattack Yoritomo, but all failed. Yoshitsune had to run away to Hiraizumi (Miyagi Pref.

Benkei's juggling Stone

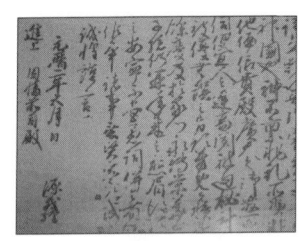

Yoshitsune's letter to Yoritomo

in northern Japan) for help from the Fujiwara family.

In 1189 in the Battle of Koromogawa, surrounded by Yoritomo's troops, Yoshitune killed his own wife, **Sato Gozen**, his 4 year daughter **Kametsuru Gozen,** and himself.

In Mampukuji temple, the draft of Yoshitsune's letter to Yoritomo "Koshigoe-jo", is exhibited together with other articles such as his faithful assistant **Benkei's** belongings.

Honjo-ji 本成寺

Official name: Ryuko-zan Honjo-ji
Sect: Nichiren-Shu
Inaugurated by Nikken in 1309
Principal icon: Sanbo Soshi
1 min. from Koshigoe Sta. on the Enoden Line
Address: 2-19-9 Koshigoe, Kamakura City, Kanagawa Pref. Tel: 0467-31-1481

The narrow street that runs parellel to the northern side of the Enoden tramway street, used to be the main street of Koshigoe village. Most of the "Ryuko-ji Rinban Hakka-ji" (the eight temples) are built along this ancient main street. One of them, Honjo-ji, can be found just 50m distance from Enoden Koshigoe station.

Kangyo-ji 勧行寺

Official name: Ryuko-zan Kangyo-ji
Sect: Nichiren-Shu
Inaugurated by Nichijitsu in 1303
Built by Onju-in Nichiyu
Principal icon: Sanbo Soshi
1 min. from Koshigoe Sta. on the Enoden Line
Address: 2-19-15 Koshigoe, Kamakura City, Kanagawa Pref. Tel: 0467-31-0382

Also one of the "Ryuko-ji Rinban Hakka-ji" eight temples, Kangyo-ji has been damaged several times by various disasters: a fire in 1683, a huge tempest in 1791 and the Great Earthquake of 1923.

The Monju Bosatsu enshrined with the principal icon, Sanbo Soshi, has another Monju Bosatsu statue in its body. This Bosatsu was found in the sea and brought home by a young fisherman. However, after that all the family members began to regularly have horrible nightmares. Becoming scared, the fisherman brought the statue to Kangyo-ji in order to have it enshrined. Strangely enough, no more bad things happened to the family after that.

The main hall's ceiling is decorated with an impressive painting of dragons.

Myoten-ji 妙典寺

Official name: Ryuko-zan Myoten-ji
Sect: Nichiren-Shu
Inaugurated by Tenmoku in 1308
Principal icon: Sanbo Soshi
Open: 9:00-18:00
3 min. from Koshigoe Sta. on the Enoden Line
Address: 2-20-5 Koshigoe, Kamakura City, Kanagawa Pref. Tel: 0467-31-1377

This is a small temple, but it has a long history related to Nichiren and even centuries earlier. Many houses have been constructed here in recent decades, so the original temples of long ago are now inconspicuous and sometimes hard to find in the narrow streets.

Myoten-ji temple is constructed in an open spot between valleys not far from Kangyo-ji temple. The monk **Tenmoku**, one of Nichiren's top nine diciples, was also the founder of Honko-ji in Zaimokuza.

Tozen-ji 東漸寺

Official name: Ryuko-zan Tozen-ji
Sect: Nichiren-Shu
Inaugurated by Nitto in 1352
Principal icon: Statue of Nichiren
Open until 17:00
3 min. from Koshigoe Sta. on the Enoden Line
Address: 2-22-13 Kashigoe, Kamakura City, Kanagawa

Pref. Tel: 0467-31-6232

Tozen-ji stands right next to Myoten-ji. The fact that five of the eight Ryuko-ji administrative temples are concentrated around here shows this very area was once the center of Koshigoe town in ancient times. **Nitto** was transferred from Hokke-kyo-ji of Nakayama (Chiba Pref.) to inaugurate this temple.

The main gate is named Yakui-mon, which means "medical care". This gate was built by a donation from an owner of a cake shop in front of Ryuko-ji. He lost his wife at a young age and wanted to mourn his beloved wife by praying for everyone's health. The temple's courtyard has many artistic stones.

Honryu-ji 本龍寺

Official name: Ryuko-zan Honryu-ji
Sect: Nichiren-Shu
Inaugurated by Nichigyo in 1302
Principal icon: Mandara of Nichiren
3 min. from Koshigoe Sta. on the Enoden Line
Address: 2-26-2 Koshigoe, Kamakura City, Kanagawa
Pref. Tel: 0467-31-1541

Honryu-ji is the oldest temple among the "Ryuko-ji Rinban Hakka-ji", the eight Ryuko-ji administrative temples. The main icon is not a statue but the inscription of the Hokkekyo sutra by Nichiren. The inaugurator, Nichigyo, was ranked next to Nichiro, who founded Myohon-ji in Omachi, so Honryu-ji officially belongs to the Myohon-ji order.

Hozen-in 宝善院

Official name: Taicho-zan Ruriko-ji Hozen-in
Sect: Shingon-Shu Daikaku-ji sect
Inaugurated by Taicho between 765-767
Principal icon: Yakushi Nyorai
7 min. from Koshigoe Sta. or Enoshima Sta. on the Enoden Line
Address: 5-13-17 Koshigoe, Kamakura City, Kanagawa
Pref. Tel: 0467-25-3238

Leaving Enoden Koshigoe station, you walk towards the hills in the northwest. At the end of a narrow sloping street, a beautiful Yakui-mon gate welcomes visitors.

This was a very prosperous temple in the Edo era and, curiously enough, also administrated many Shinto shrines in the village community. The inaugurator, **Taicho**, was from Niigata (in northern Japan) and was respected as the most virtuous priest of the province.

The principal icon, Yakushi Nyorai, is correctly called Yakushi Ruriko Nyorai. This Nyorai delivers twelve major vows to save the people from illness and cure hopeless diseases. Yakushi Nyorai raises his right hand with the palm open and holds a medicine pot with the left hand. The wooden Juichimen Kan-non has another human figure on its head. The priest Taicho cherished this Kan-non as his principal object of worship.

Hogen-ji 法源寺

Official name: Ryuko-zan Hogen-ji
Sect: Nichiren-Shu
Inaugurated by Nichigyo in 1303
Principal icon: Mandara of Nichiren
10 min. from Mejiroyama Sta. on the Shonan Monorail Line or Enoshima Sta. on the Enoden Line
Address: 5-1-17 Koshigoe, Kamakura City, Kanagawa Pref. Tel: 0467-25-3238

Nichigyo opened this temple a year after he opened Honryu-ji. The main icon, a Mandara, is a copied manuscript of Hokkekyo sutra by Nichiren. The statue of Nichiren at this temple is made of the same wood the Nichiren statue of Ryuko-ji is made of.

This temple is otherwise called "Botamochi Dera", just like Joei-ji is in Omachi. It is said that when Nichiren was on the way to the execution site, an old woman of Koshigoe village tried to offer him some rice balls. However, she tripped on a stone and fell, dropping her rice ball on the ground. Nevertheless, Nichiren ate her dirt-covered rice ball. As she was later buried in this temple, the temple started to offer rice cakes to everybody once a year on September 13.

There is another similar legend about Botamochi here.

The younger sister of the **Lady Hiki Yoshikazu** was a nun named Sajiki-ni. She also had a similar experience of offering rice-balls to Nichiren on the way to his execution. As Hogen-ji was her family temple, they began to call this temple "Botamochi-dera". The word "Botamochi" comes from Botan Mochi, a rice cake "Mochi" made of two different sorts of steamed rice paste mixed with Azuki beans. People in old times thought it looked like a Botan (peony).

Ryuko-ji 龍口寺

Official name: Jakko-zan Ryuko-ji
Sect: Nichiren-Shu
Inaugurated by Nippo in 1337
Open: 8:00-18:00
2 min. from Enoshima Sta. on the Enoden Line or 2 min. from Shonan-Enoshima Sta. on the Shonan Monorail Line
Address: 3-13-37 Katase, Fujisawa City, Kanagawa Pref. Tel: 0466-25-7357

Ryuko-ji is built on the legendary site where a miraculous bolt of lightning saved Nichiren's life in 1271. By then, Nichiren had become very popular for his preaching, and his proven prediction about a foreign invasion. (In 1264, Japan had received a diplomatic letter from the Mongolian Emperor threatening to attack them.)

On September 12 in 1271, **Nichiren** was arrested by Kamakura Shogun, **Hojo Tokimune** and sentenced to death. The entourage arrived at Tatsunokuchi near Enoshima for the execution, and Nichiren, after telling his followers there to be grateful for his being able to die for the sake of Buddha's teaching, began to chant his Hokkekyo sutra. His followers joined him.

The executioner, **Echi-no-Saburo**, raised his sword. Then, all of a sudden, the sky and the ocean turned stormy, and lightening struck the executioner's sword, breaking it into pieces. Dizzy and terrified by the tremendously strong light, the executioners lost courage to continue their job and were about to flee the area.

Execution site of Nichiren

Nichiren, however, scolded them for leaving their prisoner alone. Witnessing the shrunken morale of these men made the governor feel that it would not be possible to continue with the execution. The Hojo government, therefore, revoked the death penalty, and exiled Nichiren to Sado Island in that year, instead.

Ryuko-ji was thus constructed on this sacred place in 1337 by Nichiren's disciple, **Nippo**. He first built a tiny hut called Shikigawa-do (Shikigawa means a mat, which Nichiren was sitting on during the incident) and posed a wooden statue of Nichiren that Nippo, himself, had sculptured..

Five storied Pagoda

In 1601, the chief priest of Ikegami Honmon-ji, **Nisson**, started the holy project of constructing a big temple on Shikigawa-do with the help of **Shimamura Uneme**, a local man and sincere believer of Nichiren, who donated a large piece of land. Thereafter, the temple began to grow little by little, and in 1818, they finally succeeded in inaugurating the main hall.

Later, in 1856, a wealthy merchant, **Konoike** of Naniwa (Osaka,) donated funds for the construction of the gate.

From its beginning until the year 1886, no priest lived in the temple. The eight Nichiren-shu temples in the area took charge of the administration of the temple by turns. These "Ryuko-ji Rinban Hakkaji", (surrounding eight temples) are Myoten-ji, Honryu-ji, Kangyo-ji, Honju-ji, Hogen-ji, Tozen-ji, Joryu-ji and Honren-ji.

Anyone is free to toll the bell

The five storied pagoda, which is the only one of this kind in the Kamakura area, was constructed by Takenaka Construction Company in 1910. Each floor is 4.5m square.

A dungeon built in the cave where Nichiren passed the night before the day of execution, is still preserved. In the dungeon, a statue of Nichiren is displayed. There is also a Busshari pagoda (tower of Buddha's ashes) that was built in 1971 on the hilltop. The cemetery of the family of Shimamura Uneme is beside the Hondo.

Dungeon of Nichiren

On September 12, the day of "Tatsuno-kuchi Honan", a commemorative ceremony is held and "Botamochi" rice cakes are given to visitors, like in Joei-ji temple in Omachi. Visitors are free to enter the bell tower and to toll the bell any time of the year.

Joryu-ji 常立寺

Official name: Ryuko-zan Joryu-ji
Sect: Nichiren-Shu
Inaugurated by Nichigo in 1532
Principal icon: Mandara of Nichiren
Open until sunset
1 min. from Enoshima Sta. on the Enoden Line
Address: 3-14-3 Katase, Fujisawa City, Kanagawa Pref. Tel: 0466-26-1911

5 Mongolians memorial monument

Joryu-ji is situated on the western side of Ryuko-ji. Sometime between 1275 and 1532, a temple called Rishu-ji of the Shingon-shu sect was built here in mourning for the people executed at Ryuko-ji, including several Mongolians.

In October 1274, **Khubilai Khan** attacked Iki and Tsushima Islands with his 30,000 warriors, and landed on Hakata in Kyushu. They severely beat the Japanese soldiers, but because of a typhoon, more than 10,000 of his soldiers drowned, and Khubilai had to withdraw. The next year (1275), Khubilai first sent a delegation of five diplomats to Japan, to demand Japan's surrender. They arrived in Kamakura in September and **Hojo Tokimune**, who was willing to fight the Mongols again, ordered them killed. The five were executed at Tatsunokuchi (now Ryuko-ji) on September 7 and buried in Risho-ji.

Later, a memorial cenotaph was built in Joryu-ji temple to mourn the Mongolian diplomats. However, it's existence was not well known until recently because Mongolia and Japan had not had

Mongolian Sumo wrestlers worshipping for their compatriots (April, 2006)

an official diplomatic relationship during the Soviet regime. Once free interchange between both countries started, a ceremony was soon organized. Well-known Grand Sumo Champions such as Asashoryu and Hakuho from Mongolia have visited this temple to attend the annual memorial service.

Honren-ji. 本蓮寺

Official name: Ryuko-zan Honren-ji
Sect: Nichiren-Shu
Inaugurated by Nisshu in 1304
Principal icon: Shakamuni Butsu, Mandara of Nichiren
Open until sunset
5 min. from Enoshima Sta. on the Enoden Line
Address: 3-4-41 Katase, Fujisawa City, Kanagawa Pref. Tel: 0466-22-9039

According to the temple's historical records, this temple was originally opened by the monk **Gigen** in the time of **Empress Suiko** (593-628) with the name of Miwa-dera. Later, in the Kamakura era, **Minamoto Yoritomo** rebuilt the main hall, a five storied pagoda and other buildings, and also changed the name of the temple to Genryuju-ji.

When Nichiren survived the execution at Tatsuno-kuchi, he came here to take a rest before being exiled to Sado Island.

In 1304, Nichiren's disciple **Nisshu**, changed the temple's sect to Nichiren-shu and changed the name to the present one.

When the Kamakura shogunate collapsed under attack by **Nitta Yoshisada** in 1333, the temple was completely burnt down. It has been rebuilt little by little, and in the Edo era, the Tokugawa Shogunate granted some land to the temple.

After the long approach, the Tokugawa crest of three hollyhock leaves can be seen on the main gate. From the stone arch bridge, we can see a pagoda on the hillside.

There is a stone monument of **Prince Munetaka**'s poetry. He wrote: "Never will we see again Katase river, since the dirty water will never get clean in this world". He was Shogun in Kamakura from age 13 to 27, but de facto only a powerless puppet. The real power was in the hands of Regent Hojo Tokiyori, and

Munekata was later replaced by Tokiyori's son, Tokimune.

Enoshima Jinja　江島神社

Hetsu-no-miya (outer) Shrine

Ho-an-den

Official name: Enoshima Jinja
Enshrined Gods: Tagitsuhime-no-Mikoto (Hetsu-no-Miya Shrine), Ichikishimahime-no-Mikoto (Nakatsu-no-Miya Shrine), Tagirihime-no-Mikoto (Okutsu-no-Miya Shrine)
Founded in 552
Virtue: wealthy life, development in art, safe navigation, prevention of automobile accidents
Annual festival: First Serpent day of April, First Boar day of October
Sub shrines: Yasaka Jinja, Akiba-sha, Inari-sha, Wadatsumi-no-Miya
15 min. from Katase Enoshima Sta. on the Odakyu Line
Address: 2-3-8 Enoshima, Fujisawa City, Kanagawa pref. Tel: 0466-22-4020

The shrine's historical records tell us that Emperor Kinmei opened the shrine in April, 552. These three Mikoto or Godesses, Tagitsuhime-no-Mikoto, Ichikishimahime-no-Mikoto and Tagirihime-no-Mikoto were popularly called "Enoshima Myojin" were widely respected as tutelary Gods of marine transportation, fishing and traffic.

The main shrine is Hetsunomiya, sacred to Tagitsuhime-no-mikoto, and was originally founded in 1206 by Minamoto Sanetomo, the 3rd Kamakura Shogun. It consists of three buildings: Haiden (oratory hall), Heiden (offerings hall) and Honden (sanctum). All were rebuilt in 1657.

To the left of the shrine is the octagonal Ho-an-den, meaning a hall to install holy objects (the structure was modeled after Yumedono of Horyuji in Nara). It is dedicated to the two famous Benten Statues, the nude Benten and the one equipped with eight arms. The nude, milk-white Benten statue measuring 54 centimeters tall, is in a half-cross-legged posture playing the lute.

The other Benten is a 59cm tall, eight armed statue. Each hand holds an ob-

Nakatsu-no-miya (middle) Shrine

Okutsu-no-miya (inner) shrine

Caves

ject such as a sword, a bow, a hoju (a Buddhist fitting with peach shaped head decor) etc.. The statue was made during the Kamakura Period.

At the Meiji Restoration of 1868, during the anti-Buddhist movement, Buddhist statues were dumped into a corner of the hall of Nakatsu-no-miya. Many parts of the statures were damaged One can find some cracks on the left arm, the left leg and the right ankle. (Open from 9:00 a.m. to 16:30. Admission: ¥200)

This shrine was built by a Buddhist Priest, En-nin, in 853 to enshrine Ichikishimahime-no-mikoto. In the courtyard, many old stone lanterns donated during the Edo era can be found. The building was restored in 1996.

Okutsu-no-miya was originally a luxurious building, but it burnt down in 1841 and was rebuilt in 1842. Enshrined here is Tagirihime-no-mikoto. Legend tells us that the Goddess usually stays in the cave down the cliff during winter. She comes up here on the first Serpent Day of April and goes back to the cave on the first Boar Day of October.

On the ceiling of the oratory, the famous "Happo-Nirami-no-Kame" (A Turtle Glaring in Eight Directions), painted by Sakai Hogetsu (1761-1829), seems to stare down at you no matter where you stand.

In the cliff on the southern side, there are two caves which can be reached by going down 220 stone steps. The caves are facing the ocean on a more natural and wilder side of the island.

The first (west) cave is 13m wide at the entrance and pierces to a depth of 145m. Roughly 100m in stands a statue of the Priest **Kukai**, and then the cave branches. The right-hand side, 39m deep, is called Kongo (diamond) Cave and the left side, 20m deep, is Taizo (womb)

Yasaka Shrine

Cave. The cave also houses Shinto deities. The three goddesses are still enshrined in the innermost recess of the right-hand cave, and Amaterasu O-mikami is in the left-hand cave. However, the cave is also filled with a number of stone-statues mostly associated with Shingon sect Buddhism,.

The second (east) cave, which is linked to the first one, is dedicated to Ryujin (the dragon God), which has long been believed to be the guardian deity for fishermen. In the far end is the statue of a fierce-looking dragon, colored green. From time to time, the artificial sound of thunder surprises visitors, although it is a bit too touristy.

Legend says that when Hojo Tokimasa, father-in-law of Yoritomo and the first Hojo Regent, visited here and prayed for the prosperity of his offspring, a dragon appeared and told him that his wishes would come true. When the dragon left, he left behind three scales, which are the origin of the Hojo crest, "Three Scales".

The caves are open from 9:00 to 17:00 year-round (9:00 to 16:00 from November through February. Admission: ¥500).

Just next to the Ho-an-den stands Yasaka Shrine. The head Yasaka Jinja Shrine is in Kyoto, and this is one of its branch shrines . The shrine worships Susano-no-mikoto, a Japanese mythological god. At the time Yasaka Shrine was founded in the ninth century, however, it was called "Gion-sha", and its purpose was to stave off epidemics in Kyoto. The epidemics were believed to have been brought by the curse of **Gozu-ten-no**, which, according to Buddhist teachings, resides in Gion Shoja (An ancient temple in India erected as a guardian deity). After Yasaka Shrine was built to appease the curse of Gozu-Ten-no, the epidemic then ravaging Kyoto died out. From then onward, people in Kyoto began to venerate this god.

The Shrine holds a grand festival on a weekend near the fourteenth of July every year. Mikoshi, or portable shrines, parade in the sea facing the opposite shore (see Koyurugi Jinja).

Ryuko Myojinsha　龍口明神社

Official name: Ryuko Myojinsha
Built in 552

Enshrined Gods: Tamayarihime-no-Mikoto
Sub-shrine: Kyoroku Inari Jinja
Virtue: Peaceful family, winning luck
Annual festival: First or second Saturday of October
5 min. from Nishi-Kamakura Sta. on the Shonan Monorail Line
Address: 1548-4 Koshigoe, Kamakura City, Kanagawa Pref.

This is a very old shrine that was first built in 552. It originally stood next to Ryuko-ji, but as it was in Fujisawa City, they moved it to the present location in 1978. Myojin is a God of water, and it appears in the shape of a dragon. This shrine also originates as a shrine worshipping a five-headed dragon that lived in the Fukazawa area (Fukazawa means deep swampland). The legend says that this five-headed dragon surrendered to Benzaiten's spiritual power and eventually married her.

During the major festival of Enoshima shrine, which is held every 60 years, the Omikoshi of Ryuko Myojinsha traditionally goes to Enoshima.

Shoren-ji　青蓮寺

Official name: Hanjo-zan Nio-in Shoren-ji
Sect: Shingon-Shu Koya-san sect
Inaugurated by Kukai (Kobo Daishi) in 819
Principal icon: Kobo Daishi
Take the bus bound for Enoshima or Tsumura from JR Ofuna Sta. west exit, and get off at Kusari Daishi bus stop. or 10 min. from Nishi-Kamakura Sta. on the Shonan Monorail Line
Address: 769 Tebiro, Kamakura City, Kanagawa Pref.
Tel: 0467-31-1352

During **Kukai**'s (**Kobo Daishi**) wanderings around eastern Japan, he stayed here in Kamakura in 819 to practice a secret ascetism. At that time, the Benten Goddess appeared and encouraged him. After he completed his ascetic training, she entrusted him with a piece of Busshari (Buddha's ashes), and disappeared into the pond. Next morning, he found the pond covered with beautiful blue lotus flowers. Shoren means blue lotus flower.

This temple is otherwise called "Kusari Daishi" (Great Monk of Chains), because the principal icon statue's legs are joined to the body with chains in order to be movable. The statue's fingernails are made of crystal. This statue is said to have been made by Kukai himself in 816 as an offering to **Emperor Saga**.

It was originally in Togaku-In of Tsurugaoka Hachiman-gu, but at the Meiji Restoration, was removed to this temple. It is not shown to the public except on January 1st and the 3rd Saturday of April.

Ofuna Kan-non-ji 大船観音寺

Official name: Bukkai-zan Ofuna Kan-non-ji
Sect: Soto-Shu
Inaugurated by Otokawa Kin-ei in 1981
Principal icon: Sei-Kan-non
Open: 9:00-17:00 (16:30 in winter)
Entrance fee: adult ¥300 children ¥100
10 min. from JR Ofuna Sta. west exit
Address: 1-5-3 Okamoto, Kamakura City, Kanagawa Pref.
Tel: 0467-43-1561

A-bomb Peace memorial monument

The most eye-catching symbol of Ofuna is the Great Kan-non, which looks down on us from the hilltop near the station.

The statue is 25.39m high, 18.57m wide and weighs 1915t. The construction of the temple was started in 1929, but was not completed until 1960, having been interrupted because of financial reasons and the wars.

In 1954, the chief priest of Eihei-ji in Fukui, **Takashina Rosen**, and his supporters established the Ofuna Kan-non Association to finish the construction and completed the work in 3 years at the cost of 35,000,000 yen.

Inside the statue, there is a ceremony hall where the statue of a Kan-non of

Bricks burned by A-bomb

Heian era, which is the temple's principal icon, is worshipped.

In the court yard, the Hiroshima Peace memorial monument stands together with the monument of bricks burned by the A-bomb and a stone lantern in which fire from the A-bomb is kept burning.

[Writers' profiles]

Kenji Kamio (神尾賢二)

Kenji Kamio has been directing films and TV documentaries for more than 30 years in Tokyo, and has recently been translating foreign books into Japanese. Living in Kamakura for 11 years, he wrote this guide hoping to provide a deeper knowledge of the city's historical treasures for visitors from abroad.

Heather Willson

Heather Willson was born in Canada, but has spent the past 34 years in Japan, mostly in Kamakura. During her work on the community paper, The Kamakura Post, and other local activities, she became very familiar with the city's sights and events, and now considers Kamakura her "home for life"

An English Guide to Kamakura's Temples & Shrines
Copyright©2008 by Kenji Kamio and Heather Willson
Printed in Japan
ISBN978-4-8461-0811-3 C0026
RYOKUFU SHUPPAN,INC.,2-17-5 Hongo Bunkyou-ku Tokyo 113-0033 Japan

An English Guide to Kamakura's Temples & Shrines

2008年8月30日	初版第1刷発行	定価 1500 円＋税
2008年9月30日	初版第2刷発行	
2014年6月10日	初版第3刷発行	

著 者　神尾賢二　ヘザー・ウイルソン ©
発行者　高須次郎
発行所　緑風出版
　　　　〒113-0033　東京都文京区本郷 2-17-5　ツイン壱岐坂
　　　　［電話］03-3812-9420　［FAX］03-3812-7262
　　　　［E-mail］info@ryokufu.com
　　　　［郵便振替］00100-9-30776
　　　　［URL］http://www.ryokufu.com/

装　幀	堀内朝彦		
制　作	R 企画	印　刷	シナノ・巣鴨美術印刷
製　本	シナノ	用　紙	大宝紙業　　　　　E700

〈検印廃止〉乱丁・落丁は送料小社負担でお取り替えします。
本書の無断複写（コピー）は著作権法上の例外を除き禁じられています。なお、複写など著作物の利用などのお問い合わせは日本出版著作権協会（03-3812-9424）までお願いいたします。

Printed in Japan　　　　　　　　　　　　　ISBN978-4-8461-0811-3　C0026

JPCA 日本出版著作権協会
http://www.e-jpca.com/

＊本書は日本出版著作権協会（JPCA）が委託管理する著作物です。
　本書の無断複写などは著作権法上での例外を除き禁じられています。複写（コピー）・複製、その他著作物の利用については事前に日本出版著作権協会（電話 03-3812-9424, e-mail:info@e-jpca.com）の許諾を得てください。